Study Guide

Managing Human Resources

FIFTEENTH EDITION

George Bohlander
Professor Emeritus of Management,
Arizona State University

Scott Snell
Professor of Business Administration,
University of Virginia

Prepared by

Satish P. Deshpande
Western Michigan University

SOUTH-WESTERN
CENGAGE Learning

Australia • Brazil • Japan • Korea • Mexico • Singapore • Spain • United Kingdom • United States

SOUTH-WESTERN
CENGAGE Learning

ISBN-13: 978-0-324-59261-0
ISBN-10: 0-324-59261-2

South-Western Cengage Learning
5191 Natorp Boulevard
Mason, OH 45040
USA

Printed in the United States of America
1 2 3 4 5 6 7 11 10 09

Table of Contents

PREFACE

The student Study Guide that accompanies the 15th Edition of *Managing Human Resources* by Bohlander & Snell offers you the motivation to do well in this course. The objective of the student Study Guide is to increase your understanding of human resources management theory and concepts with a number of review features.

Learning Objectives. After you have read the chapter in the text, read the Learning Objectives to review what you should have learned from the chapter.

Chapter Summary. The Chapter Summary is prepared in conjunction with the learning objectives. Read and study the Chapter Summary carefully. Review any concepts in the text that you did not completely understand.

Self-Test Questions. The Self-Test section includes three separate self-test exercises—**Multiple Choice** questions, **True/False** questions, and a **Definition Review** in the form of matching questions. Test questions are new and revised, and the Multiple Choice questions include real-life applications questions to improve your understanding of the business of human resource management as it relates to theoretical concepts. **Internet exercises** will add to your Internet researching skills, and a **How To** section will help improve your understanding of the human resources function as it applies to recruitment, selection, orientation, and training, with a focus on continuous improvement through the creation of workforce diversity.

When reading and studying the textbook, use the opportunity to apply and integrate the knowledge you have gained to answer the questions that appear in this Study Guide.

Answers. The answers to all the Multiple Choice, True/False, and Definition Review questions are found at the end of each chapter. Check your answers only after you have answered all of the questions. Reviewing any incorrect answers may suggest the need for further review of the text material. You can easily find the material in the textbook by using the learning objective icon that appears with each Multiple Choice and True/False question.

Have a great semester.

PART ONE

Human Resources Management in Perspective

CHAPTER

1

THE CHALLENGE OF HUMAN RESOURCES MANAGEMENT

As a student you will learn how firms gain sustainable competitive advantage with and through people. You will be able to comprehend the concept of globalization and the impact it is having on human resources (HR) management. This awareness will provide a perspective with which to interpret current practices, problems, and issues more clearly. Chapter 1 is designed to make you aware of the challenges of human resources management that you will encounter in the work environment. In reading this chapter you will be able to understand how information technology challenges managers and employees. Also, you will become acquainted with the growing body of knowledge in the field. In this chapter, you will learn about the importance of change management, about the tools that are used by human resources managers (such as the development of intellectual capital), and about the ways total quality management (TQM) and reengineering challenge human resources systems. You will be able to learn the roles and competencies required by human resources managers. Finally, you will be able to understand the impact of cost pressures on human resources policies and the pertinence of changing demographics and employee concerns to human resources management.

LEARNING OBJECTIVES

After studying this chapter, you should be able to

1 Identify how firms gain sustainable competitive advantage through people.

2 Explain how globalization is influencing human resources management.

3 Describe the impact of information technology on managing people.

4 Identify the importance of change management.

5 Describe HR's role in developing intellectual capital.

6 Explain how TQM, Six Sigma, and reengineering affect HR systems.

7 Discuss how cost pressures affect HR policies.

8 Discuss the primary demographic and employee concerns pertaining to HRM.

9 Provide examples of the roles and competencies of today's HR managers.

CHAPTER SUMMARY RELATING TO LEARNING OBJECTIVES

1 People have always been central to organizations, but their strategic importance is growing in today's knowledge-based industries. An organization's success increasingly depends on the knowledge, skills, and abilities of employees.

2 Globalization influences approximately 70 to 85 percent of the U.S. economy and affects the free flow of trade among countries. This influences the number and kinds of jobs that are available and requires that organizations balance a complicated set of issues related to managing people working under business conditions in different geographies, cultures, and legal environments. Human resources functions such as staffing, training, compensation, and the like have to be adjusted to take into account these differences.

3 Advanced technology has tended to reduce the number of jobs that require little skill and to increase the number of jobs that require considerable skill, a shift we refer to as moving from touch labor to knowledge workers. This displaces some employees and requires that others be retrained. In addition, information technology has influenced human resources management through human resources information systems (HRIS) that streamline HR processes, make information more readily available to managers and employees, and enable HR departments to focus on the firm's strategies.

4 Both proactive and reactive change initiatives require human resources managers to work with line managers and executives to create a vision for the future, establish an architecture that enables change, and communicate with employees about the processes of change.

5 In order to "compete through people," organizations have to do a good job of managing human capital; the knowledge, skills, and capabilities that have value to organizations. Managers must develop strategies for identifying, recruiting, and hiring the best talent available; for developing these employees in ways that are firm-specific; for helping them to generate new ideas and generalize them through the company; for encouraging information sharing; and for rewarding collaboration and teamwork.

6 In order to respond to customer needs better, faster, and more cheaply, organizations have instituted total-quality management (TQM), Six Sigma, and reengineering programs. Each of these programs requires that human resources be involved in changing work processes, training, job design, compensation, and the like. Human resources issues also arise when communicating with employees about the new work systems, just as with any change initiative. Better business thinking builds more strategic HR thinking.

7 In order to contain costs, organizations have been downsizing, outsourcing, offshoring, leasing employees, and enhancing productivity. Human resources' role is to maintain the relationship between a company and its employees, while implementing various changes.

8 The workforce is becoming increasingly diverse and organizations are doing more to address employee concerns and to maximize the benefit of different kinds of employees. Demographic changes, social and cultural differences, and changing attitudes toward work can provide rich sources of variety for organizations. But to benefit from diversity, managers need to recognize the potential concerns of employees and make certain that the exchange between the organization and employees is mutually beneficial.

9 In working with line managers to address the organization's challenges, HR managers play a number of important roles—they are called on for advice and ethics counsel, for various service activities, for policy formulation and implementation, and for employee advocacy. To perform these roles effectively, human resources managers must contribute business competencies, state-of-the-art human resources competencies, and change-management competencies. Ultimately, managing people is rarely the exclusive responsibility of the human resources function. Every manager's job is managing people. Consequently, successful companies combine the expertise of human resources specialists with the experience of line managers to develop and utilize the talents of employees to their greatest potential.

REVIEW QUESTIONS

Multiple Choice

Choose the letter of the word or phrase that best completes each statement.

1

_______ 1. Successful organizations are particularly adept at bringing together different kinds of people to achieve a common purpose which is the essence of
- a. quality circles.
- b. total quality management.
- c. human resources management (HRM).
- d. Six Sigma.

2

_______ 2. In order to grow and prosper, many companies are seeking business opportunities in
- a. global markets.
- b. industrial markets.
- c. domestic operations.
- d. employment markets.

2

_______ 3. United State's biggest trading gap is with
- a. China
- b. India
- c. Japan
- d. Canada.

2

_______ 4. Approximately what percentage of the U.S. economy is affected by international competition?
- a. 25-40
- b. 40-55
- c. 55-70
- d. 70-85

2

_______ 5. The first major trade agreement of the twentieth century, which established rules and guidelines for global commerce between nations and groups of nations, is called
- a. World Market Operations.
- b. Uniform Trade of Commerce.
- c. North American Free Trade Agreement.
- d. General Agreement on Tariffs and Trade (GATT).

2 ______ 6. Concerns that people in developing economies and the world's environment are being exploited by companies in richer, more developed countries, coupled with numerous scandals plaguing U.S. corporations, have led to a new focus on
a. environmental trade protection.
b. uniform commerce and trade.
c. fair trade protection.
d. corporate social responsibility.

2 ______ 7. When managers talk about "going global," they have to balance a complicated set of issues related to different
a. trade pacts, economic conditions, and customs.
b. employment laws, labor unions, and cultural distinctions.
c. trade customs, protection laws, tariffs, and trade agreements.
d. geographies, cultures, and employment laws.

3 ______ 8. The organizational challenge of the new millennium is
a. e-commerce.
b. tariffs and trade.
c. industrial marketing.
d. uniform trade practice.

3 ______ 9. The introduction of advanced technology tends to increase the number of jobs that require
a. less skill and knowledge.
b. less know-how and work applications.
c. greater responsibility with less pay.
d. considerable skill.

3 ______ 10. When employee responsibilities expand to include a richer array of activities such as planning, decision making, and problem solving, the transformation has been referred to as
a. collective bargaining.
b. human resources information systems.
c. job enrichment.
d. "knowledge work."

3 ______ 11. The most central use of technology in HRM is an organization's
a. human resources information system (HRIS).
b. collective bargaining process.
c. Six Sigma program.
d. HR outsourcing program.

3

_______ 12. HRIS can be a potent weapon for
a. lowering administrative costs.
b. increasing productivity.
c. speeding up response times.
d. all of the above.

3

_______ 13. The first step in choosing an HRIS is for HR personnel to evaluate the
a. costs based on average salaries.
b. HR hours.
c. hours of increased productivity.
d. biggest "headaches" they experience.

3

_______ 14. When an effective HRIS is implemented, perhaps the biggest advantage gained is that HR personnel are able to concentrate more effectively on the firm's
a. strategic direction.
b. collective bargaining process.
c. job enlargement program.
d. job enrichment program.

4

_______ 15. Paramount to a firm's success is the ability to
a. utilize the Theory X style of management.
b. keep the union out.
c. use traditional means of management.
d. manage change.

4

_______ 16. The means organizations are using to modify the way they operate in order to be more successful are programs focused on
a. total quality.
b. continuous improvement.
c. reengineering.
d. all of the above.

4

_______ 17. When external forces have already affected an organization's performance, the change is
a. proactive.
b. combative.
c. disengaging.
d. reactive.

4 _______ 18. To manage change, executives and managers, including those in HR, have to
a. envision the future.
b. communicate their vision of the future to employees.
c. develop the capability to execute by reorganizing people and reallocating assets.
d. do all of the above.

4 _______ 19. Which of the following is not a key element of change-management planning?
a. link change to business strategy.
b. engage key employees early.
c. lead clearly, unequivocally, and consistently.
d. Declare victory soon.

5 _______ 20. The economic value of knowledge, skills, and capabilities describes
a. intellectual property rights.
b. human capital.
c. collective bargaining.
d. labor law.

5 _______ 21. Programs used to complement staffing practices to provide skill enhancement, particularly in areas that cannot be transferred to another company if an employee should leave, are called
a. orientation programs.
b. recruitment programs.
c. training programs.
d. selection programs.

6 _______ 22. A set of principles and practices whose core ideas include understanding customer needs, doing things right the first time, and striving for continuous improvement is
a. Total Quality Management (TQM).
b. Collective Bargaining.
c. Six Sigma.
d. Intellectual Capital.

6

_______ 23. A more systematic approach to quality, which includes major changes in management philosophy and HR programs, is called
a. Total Quality Management (TQM).
b. Collective Bargaining.
c. Intellectual Capital.
d. Six Sigma.

6

_______24. TQM techniques were developed in the mid-1040s by
a. Peter Drucker
b. Jack Welch
c. W. Edward Deming
d. Peter Chambers

6

_______ 25. The fundamental rethinking and radical redesign of business processes to achieve dramatic improvements in cost, quality, service, and speed is referred to as
a. reengineering.
b. total quality management.
c. proactive management.
d. Six Sigma.

7

_______ 26. The planned elimination of jobs is termed
a. downsizing.
b. economic growth.
c. Six Sigma.
d. proactive management.

7

_______ 27. Hiring someone outside the company to perform tasks that could be done internally is referred to as
a. outsourcing.
b. employment leasing.
c. offshoring.
d. Six Sigma.

7

_______ 28. The controversial practice of moving jobs overseas is referred to as
a. subcontracting.
b. offshoring.
c. employee leasing.
d. outsourcing.

8 ______ 29. Being acutely aware of characteristics *common* to employees while also managing these employees as *individuals* is referred to as
a. Six Sigma.
b. outsourcing.
c. collective bargaining.
d. managing diversity.

8 ______ 30. A major activity of an HR Manager is to listen to employee concerns and represent their needs to managers. This role is referred to as
a. advise and counsel.
b. service.
c. policy formulation and implementation.
d. employee advocacy.

True/False

Identify the following statements as True or False.

1 ______ 1. The term *human resources* implies that people have capabilities that drive organizational performance (along with other resources such as money, materials, and information).

2 ______ 2. Globalization is something of interest to only large firms.

2 ______ 3. HR personnel are not responsible for implementing training programs and development opportunities to enhance managers' understanding of foreign cultures and practices.

3 ______ 4. Technology, transportation, communications, and utilities industries tend to spend the least on training.

3 ______ 5. Information technology has changed the face of HRM in the United States and abroad.

3 ______ 6. All sorts of routine HR activities, from front to back, have seen some sort of automation.

3 _______ 7. Companies are now using software to recruit, screen, and pre-test applicants online before hiring them.

4 _______ 8. In highly competitive environments, where competition is global and innovation is continuous, change has become a core competency of organizations.

4 _______ 9. Over 90% percent of organizations polled said that they have some form of change initiative going on in their organizations.

5 _______ 10. Human capital is tangible and can be managed the way organizations manage jobs, products, and technologies.

5 _______ 11. The most highly valued intelligence tends to be associated with competencies and capabilities that are taught.

5 _______ 12. Skill-based pay rewards employees for each new class of jobs they are capable of performing.

6 _______ 13. Total Quality Management techniques were developed in the mid-1940s by Dr. W. Edward Deming after studying Japanese companies rebuilding following World War II.

7 _______ 14. Organizations are taking many approaches to lowering labor-related costs, including employee leasing, in an attempt to achieve productivity enhancements.

7 _______ 15. In the largest U.S. firms, most of the jobs lost in the last decade have been line workers' jobs.

7 _______ 16. Downsizing is still being regarded as a short-term fix when times are tough.

7 _______ 17. Over the past 25 years, the employment relationship between companies and employees has shifted from relationship-based to transactional-based.

7 _______ 18. Organizations can increase productivity either by reducing the inputs (the cost approach) or by increasing the amount that employees produce, by adding more human and/or physical capital to the process.

8 _______ 19. In New Mexico and Texas minorities outnumber non-Hispanic whites.

8 _______ 20. Some of the fastest-growing sectors of employment over the past few decades have been in areas requiring less education.

8 _______ 21. Employees today are more likely to define their personal success only in terms of financial gains.

8 _______ 22. A Conference Board survey of companies with family-friendly programs found that companies acknowledge that childless employees harbor resentment against employees with children who are able to take advantage of these programs.

9 _______ 23. Human resources managers are a resource to whom managers can turn for policy interpretation.

9 _______ 24. One enduring role of HR managers is to serve as an employee advocate—listening to the employees' concerns and representing their needs to managers.

9 _______ 25. HR professionals are not required to understand the economic and financial capabilities of their organization.

Matching

Match each term with the proper definition.

Terms

a. corporate social responsibility
b. downsizing
c. employee leasing
d. globalization
e. human capital
f. human resources information system
g. human resources management (HRM)
h. knowledge workers
i. managing diversity
j. outsourcing
k. offshoring
l. proactive change
m. reactive change
n. reengineering
o. Six Sigma
p. total quality management (TQM)

Definitions

_______ 1. employees whose responsibilities are expanded to include a richer array of activities such as planning, decision-making, and problem solving

_______ 2. change that occurs after external forces have already affected performance

_______ 3. represents the knowledge, skills, and capabilities of individuals that have economic value to an organization

_______ 4. set of principles and practices whose core ideas include understanding customer needs, doing things right the first time, and striving for continuous improvement

_______ 5. contracting outside the organization to have work done that formerly was done by internal employees

_______ 6. being aware of characteristics common to employees, while managing employees as individuals

_______ 7. trend toward opening up foreign markets to international trade and investment

_______ 8. change initiated by managers to take advantage of targeted opportunities

_______ 9. the planned elimination of jobs within the organization

_______ 10. computerized system that provides current and accurate data for purposes of control and decision making

_______ 11. process of dismissing employees who are then hired by a leasing company and contracting with that company to lease back the employees

_______ 12. the fundamental rethinking and radical redesign of business processes to achieve dramatic improvements in cost, quality, service, and speed

_______ 13. good citizenship

_______ 14. the process of bringing together different kinds of people to achieve a common purpose

_______ 15. moving jobs overseas

_______ 16. a process used to translate customer needs into a set of optimal tasks that are performed in concert with one another

Internet Exercises

List the functions of Human Resources Management from the following website: http://www.managementhelp.org/hr_mgmnt/hr_mgmnt.htm.

How can U.S. firms do business in India?
http://www.buyusa.gov/india/en/motm.html

How to Develop a Working Knowledge

In developing a working knowledge, you should focus on a multiskilled approach to prepare yourself for the job market. It is important to have good communication skills, computer skills, and decision-making and problem-solving skills.

Your working knowledge should be integrated with the core competencies of the organization. The core competencies should be part of the orientation and training you receive when you join an organization. These competencies, along with an emphasis on a customer-driven approach, should provide a competitive edge for the firm. Everyone in the firm should understand and adhere to the cultural values of the organization as well as its philosophy of management. Each organization has its own management style, and you should recognize this and adapt to it. You should position yourself on a career track for advancement in the organization and take advantage of growth opportunities when they are available.

SOLUTIONS

Multiple Choice:	True/False:	Matching:
1. c	1. True	1. h
2. a	2. False	2. m
3. a	3. False	3. e
4. d	4. False	4. p
5. d	5. True	5. j
6. d	6. True	6. i
7. d	7. True	7. d
8. a	8. True	8. l
9. d	9. False	9. b
10. d	10. False	10. f
11. a	11. False	11. c
12. d	12. True	12. n
13. d	13. True	13. a
14. a	14. True	14. g
15. d	15. False	15. k
16. d	16. False	16. o
17. d	17. True	
18. d	18. True	
19. d	19. True	
20. b	20. False	
21. c	21. False	
22. a	22. True	
23. d	23. True	
24. c	24. True	
25. a	25. False	
26. a		
27. a		
28. b		
29. d		
30. d		

False Statements Made True

2. Globalization is something of interest **not just** to large firms.
3. HR personnel are **frequently** responsible for implementing training programs and development opportunities to enhance managers' understanding of foreign cultures and practices.
4. Technology, transportation, communications, and utilities industries tend to spend the **most** on training.
9. Over **eighty** percent of organizations polled said that they have some form of change initiative going on in their organizations.
10. Human capital is **intangible and elusive and cannot** be managed the way organizations manage jobs, products, and technologies.
11. The most highly valued intelligence tends to be associated with competencies and capabilities that are **learned from experience and are not easily taught**.
15. In the largest U.S. firms, most of the jobs lost in the last decade have been **white-collar jobs**.
16. Downsizing is **no longer** being regarded as a short-term fix when times are tough.
20. Some of the fastest-growing sectors of employment over the past few decades have been in areas requiring **higher levels of** education.
21. Employees today are **less** likely to define their personal success only in terms of financial gains.
25. HR professionals are **required** to understand the economic and financial capabilities of their organization.

CHAPTER

2

STRATEGY AND HUMAN RESOURCES PLANNING

In this chapter you will understand how human resources planning and strategy efforts should be integrated. You will understand various stages of the strategic management process. You will comprehend the importance of internal resource analysis and have knowledge of basic tools of human resource forecasting. You will learn the importance of formulating and implementing the appropriate strategies. You will also recognize methods for assessing and measuring the effectiveness of a firm's strategy.

LEARNING OBJECTIVES

After studying this chapter, you should be able to

1. Understand how an organization's competitive environment influences its strategic planning.
2. Understand why it's important for an organization to do an internal resource analysis.
3. Describe the basic tools for human resources forecasting.
4. Explain the linkages between competitive strategies and HR.
5. Understand what's required for a firm to successfully implement a strategy.
6. Recognize the methods for assessing and measuring the effectiveness of a firm's strategy.

CHAPTER SUMMARY RELATING TO LEARNING OBJECTIVES

1 Strategic human resources management (SHRM) integrates strategic planning and HR planning. It can be thought of as the pattern of human resources deployments and activities that enable an organization to achieve its strategic goals. HR planning and strategies become especially critical when organizations consider global strategies, including mergers, joint ventures, offshoring, the relocation of plants, product innovations, and downsizing, or when dramatic shifts in the composition of the labor force are occurring. Analyzing the firm's competitive environment is central to strategic planning. The competitive environment includes the specific organizations with which the firm interacts. Firms analyze the competitive environment in order to adapt to or influence the nature of competition.

2 Conducting an internal analysis to gauge the firm's strengths and weaknesses involves looking at the firm's "three Cs"—its culture, capabilities, and composition. An internal analysis enables strategic decision makers to inventory the organization's skills and resources as well as their performance levels.

3 An organization's success increasingly depends on the knowledge, skills, and abilities of employees, particularly as they help establish a set of core capabilities that distinguish an organization from its competitors. When employees' talents are valuable, rare, difficult to imitate, and organized, a firm can achieve a sustained competitive advantage through its people. HRP is a systematic process that involves forecasting demand for labor, performing supply analysis, and balancing supply and demand considerations. Forecasting demand requires using either quantitative or qualitative methods to identify the number and type of people needed to meet organizational objectives. Supply analysis involves determining whether sufficient employees are available within the organization to meet demand and whether potential employees are available on the job market.

4 As organizations plan for their future, top management and strategic planners must recognize that strategic-planning decisions affect—and are affected by—HR functions. On the one hand, HRP plays a reactive role in making certain the right number and type of employees are available to implement a chosen business plan. On the other hand, HRP can proactively identify and initiate programs needed to develop organizational capabilities upon which future strategies can be built. HRP and strategic planning tend to be most effective when there is a reciprocal relationship between the two processes.

5 Formulating an HR strategy is only half of the HR battle; this strategy must also be implemented. Employment forecasts must be reconciled against the internal and external supplied of labor the firm faces. This can include having current employees work overtime, hiring full –time, part-time, or contract employees, downsizing,

outsourcing, and offshoring. If there is a labor shortage, the firm might have to reformulate its long-and short-term strategic plans.

6 Firms need to establish a set of parameters that focus on the "desired outcomes" of strategic planning, as well as the metrics they will use to monitor how well the firm delivers against those outcomes. Issues of measurement, benchmarking, alignment, fit, and flexibility are central to the evaluation process. Firms use benchmarking, strategy mapping, and the Balanced Scorecard (BSC) as tools to gauge outcomes.

REVIEW QUESTIONS

Multiple Choice

Choose the letter of the word or phrase that best completes each statement.

1 _______ 1. A set of procedures for making decisions about the organization's long-term goals and strategies involves
   a. strategic planning.
   b. human resources planning (HRP).
   c. succession planning.
   d. comprehensive planning.

1 _______ 2. The process of anticipating and making provisions for the movement of people into, within, and out of an organization is
   a. succession planning.
   b. human resources planning (HRP).
   c. strategic planning.
   d. comprehensive planning.

1 _______ 3. The combination of strategic planning and HR planning is
   a. value creation.
   b. strategic vision.
   c. strategic human resources management (SHRM).
   d. succession planning.

1 _______ 4. The first step in strategic planning is establishing
   a. a mission.
   b. a vision.
   c. values for the organization.
   d. all of the above.

1 _______ 5. The strong enduring beliefs and principles that the company uses as a foundation for its decisions are its
a. core values.
b. strategies.
c. operating facilities.
d. innovations.

1 _______ 6. The second component of the strategic management process is
a. analysis of internal opportunities.
b. analysis of external opportunities and threats.
c. its external audits.
d. the organization's external component.

1 _______ 7. The systematic monitoring of the major external forces influencing the organization is
a. environmental scanning.
b. human resources planning.
c. strategic planning.
d. organizational analysis.

2 _______ 8. Integrated skills and knowledge sets within an organization that distinguish it from its competitors and deliver value to customers are its
a. operating plans.
b. strategic plans.
c. core capabilities.
d. objectives.

2 _______ 9. Which of the following programs are designed to motivate and spark creativity of workers?
a. empowerment programs.
b. total quality initiatives.
c. continuous improvement efforts.
d. all of the above.

2 _______ 10. Companies tend to make long-term commitments to these employees, investing in their continuous training and development and perhaps giving them an equity stake in the organization.
a. submarginal employees
b. operating employees
c. strategic knowledge Workers
d. management personnel

2 _______ 11. This group of individuals has skills that are unique but frequently

not directly related to a company's core strategy.
a. Core Knowledge Workers
b. Alliance Partners
c. operating employees
d. management personnel

3 _______ 12. What ultimately determines which forecasting technique will be used within an organization?
a. organizational demands.
b. staffing tables.
c. replacement charts.
d. skill inventories.

3 _______ 13. One example of a quantitative approach to forecasting that relies on a single factor is
a. Markov analysis.
b. staffing tables.
c. replacement charts.
d. trend analysis.

3 _______ 14. The opinions (judgments) of supervisors, department managers, experts, or others knowledgeable about the organization's future employment needs are
a. management forecasts.
b. core competencies.
c. strategic visions.
d. value creations.

3 _______ 15. Graphic representations of all organizational jobs, along with the numbers of employees currently occupying those jobs (and perhaps future employment requirements derived from demand forecasts), are
a. replacement charts.
b. skill inventories.
c. staffing tables.
d. organization charts.

3

_______ 16. An analysis that shows the percentage (and actual number) of employees who remain in each job from one year to the next as well as the proportions of those who are promoted, demoted, transferred, or exit the organization is called
a. trend analysis.
b. Markov analysis.
c. SWOT analysis.
d. core analysis.

3

_______ 17. A technique that lists each employee's education, past work experience, vocational interests, specific abilities and skills, compensation history, and job tenure is called
a. replacement charts.
b. Markov analysis.
c. value creation.
d. skill inventories.

3

_______ 18. Both skill and management inventories—broadly referred to as talent inventories—can be used to develop employee
a. core values.
b. core competencies.
c. organizational capability.
d. replacement charts.

3

_______ 19. The process of identifying, developing, and tracking key individuals so that they may eventually assume top-level positions is
a. strategic planning.
b. management planning.
c. succession planning.
d. human resources planning.

4

_______ 20. A comparison of strengths, weaknesses, opportunities, and threats normally is referred to as a
a. SWOT analysis.
b. Markov analysis.
c. trend analysis.
d. economic forecast.

4

_______ 21. Sometimes firms do not acquire or merge with another firm, but instead pursue cooperative strategies such as a
a. partnership.
b. takeover.
c. strategic alliance.
d. missionary statement.

4

_______ 22. A strategy based on high product quality, innovative features, speed to market, or superior service is a
a. realignment strategy.
b. differentiation strategy.
c. human resources plan.
d. strategic plan.

5

_______ 23. When forecasts show a surplus of employees, organizations may
a. restrict hiring.
b. reduce work hours.
c. consider layoffs.
d. all of the above.

5

_______ 24. A gradual reduction of employees through resignations, retirements and deaths is called
a. attrition.
b. outsourcing.
c. layoffs.
d. offshoring.

6

_______ 25. The process of identifying "best practices" in a given area—say, productivity, logistics, brand management, training, etc.—and then comparing your practices and performance to those of other companies is
a. benchmarking.
b. strategy mapping.
c. strategic planning.
d. skill inventories.

6 _______ 26. According to Mark Huselid, a competitive advantage is based on a unique combination of a company's human capital, strategy, and
a. Internal fit
b. skills inventory
c. core capabilities
d. organizational flexibility

6 _______ 27. One of the most enthusiastically adopted tools for mapping a firm's strategy in order to ensure strategic alignment is the
a. trend analysis.
b. Markov analysis.
c. Balanced Scorecard (BSC).
d. SWOT analysis.

6 _______ 28. The four related cells of the Balanced Scorecard are financial, customer, process, and
a. People
b. resources
c. learning
d. capacity.

6 _______ 29. What kind of flexibility occurs through rapid reallocation of resources to new or changing needs?
a. coordination flexibility
b. resource flexibility
c. capability flexibility
d. planning flexibility.

6 _______ 30. What kind of flexibility occurs as a result of having people who can do many different things in different ways?
a. coordination flexibility
b. resource flexibility
c. capability flexibility
d. planning flexibility.

True/False

Identify the following statements as True or False.

1 _______ 1. Dramatic shifts in the composition of the labor force require that managers become less involved in planning.

1 _______ 2. The vision is the basic purpose of the organization, as well as its scope of operations.

1 _______ 3. Although the terms *mission* and *vision* often are used interchangeably, the mission statement ideally clarifies the long-term direction of the company and its strategic intent.

1 _______ 4. While there are many factors in the general environment that may influence strategic decisions, analysis of the firm's competitive environment is central to strategic planning.

1 _______ 5. One of the most important assessments a firm can make is identifying the needs of its employees.

1 _______ 6. At times, the biggest opportunity or threat in an industry comes from direct competition.

1 _______ 7. According to the U.S. Census Bureau, employment growth will continue to be concentrated in the manufacturing sector.

1 _______ 8. According to the U.S. Census Bureau, between 2006-2016, youths (16-24 years old) will see their share of the labor force fall.

2 _______ 9. Because managers increasingly understand that employee-oriented cultures are critical to success, they often conduct cultural audits to examine the attitudes and beliefs of the workforce as well as the activities they engage in.

2 _______ 10. In many cases, products are a key resource that underlies a firm's core capabilities.

2 _______ 11. People are a source of competitive advantage when employee capabilities and contributions can be copied by others.

2 _______ 12. Skill groups in any given organization can be classified according to the degree to which they create strategic value and are unique to the organization.

2 _______ 13. Contract laborers have skills that are quite valuable to a company, but not particularly unique.

3 _______ 14. Ideally forecasting should use only qualitative methods.

3 _______ 15. Forecasting is frequently more a science than an art.

3 _______ 16. Qualitative approaches to forecasting are more statistical than quantitative approaches.

3 _______ 17. A qualitative forecasting method, the Delphi technique, attempts to decrease the subjectivity of forecasts by soliciting and summarizing the judgments of a pre-selected group of individuals.

3 _______ 18. Ideally, forecasting should include the use of both quantitative and qualitative approaches.

4 _______ 19. SWOT analysis helps executives summarize the major facts and forecasts derived from the external and internal analyses.

4 _______ 20. Some estimates suggest that only about 50 percent of all mergers achieve their objectives (measured by return on investment, shareholder value, and the like).

4 _______ 21. Companies can increase customer value by either decreasing costs to customers or increasing their benefits (or some combination).

5 _______ 22. In the case of unionized organizations, the criteria for determining an employee's eligibility for layoff are typically set forth in the union agreement.

6 _______ 23. The target company for benchmarking needs to be a competitor.

6 _______ 24. Resource flexibility occurs through rapid reallocation of resources to new or changing needs.

6 _______ 25. Resource flexibility results from having people who can do many different things in different ways.

Matching

Match each term with the proper definition.

Terms

a. benchmarking
b. core capabilities
c. core values
d. cultural audits
e. environmental scanning
f. human resources planning (HRP)
g. management forecasts
h. Markov analysis
i. mission
j. organizational capability
k. replacement charts
l. skill inventories
m. staffing tables
n. strategic HRM
o. strategic planning
p. strategic vision
q. succession planning
r. SWOT analysis
s. trend analysis
t. value creation
u. Balanced Scorecard (BSC)
v. human capital readiness

Definitions

_______ 1. integrated knowledge sets within an organization that distinguish it from its competitors and deliver value to customers

_______ 2. the basic purpose of the organization as well as its scope of operations

_______ 3. the procedures for making decisions about the organization's long-term goals and strategies

_______ 4. the process of comparing the organization's processes and practices with those of other companies

_______ 5. the systematic monitoring of the major external forces influencing the organization

_______ 6. the opinions (judgments) of supervisors, department managers, experts, or others knowledgeable about the organization's future employment needs

_______ 7. graphic representations of all organizational jobs, along with the numbers of employees currently occupying those jobs (and future employment requirements)

_______ 8. process of identifying, developing, and tracking key individuals for executive positions

_______ 9. files of personnel education, experience, interests, skills, etc., that allow managers to quickly match job openings with employee backgrounds

_______ 10. process of anticipating and making provisions for the movement of people into, within, and out of an organization

_______ 11. listings of current job holders and persons who are potential replacements if an opening occurs

_______ 12. a comparison of strengths, weaknesses, opportunities, and threats for strategy formulation purposes

_______ 13. a quantitative approach to forecasting labor demand based on an organization index such as sales

_______ 14. method for tracking the pattern of employee movements through various jobs

_______ 15. the pattern of human resources deployments and activities that enable an organization to achieve its strategic goals

_______ 16. the strong enduring beliefs and principles that the company uses as a foundation for its decisions

_______ 17. a statement about the direction the company is taking and what it can become in the future; clarifies the long-term direction of the company and its strategic intent

_______ 18. audits of the culture and quality of work life in an organization

_______ 19. capacity of the organization to act and change in pursuit of sustainable competitive advantage

_______20. what the firm adds to a product or service by virtue of making it; the amount of benefits provided by the product or service once the costs of making it are subtracted

_______21. A tool for mapping a firm's strategy in order to ensure strategic alignment.

_______22. what the firm can understand once both the supply and demand for employee skills, talent, and know-how.

Internet Exercises

Workforce planning is a systematic approach to anticipating staffing needs and determining what activity should be undertaken to meet these needs. What does this multistep process involve?
http://www.suite101.com/article.cfm/human_resources/89522

Why is benchmarking a continual process?
http://www.pwc.com/extweb/service.nsf/docid/D70EBAA20A19F91F80256C220032149
7

How to Write a Resume and Search for a Job

It is important to prepare and market yourself for a job before graduating from your educational institution. Most colleges and universities have a placement office, and you should contact this office before graduation. Services provided by this office include the following:

- resume writing
- portfolio development
- interview coaching
- tapping the hidden job market
- job searching using the Internet

Before graduation you should inquire about cooperative education to gain field experience through an internship, an externship, a practicum, a clinical placement, and other job-related experiences. It is difficult for a student to market a degree without any field experience.

You should attend workshops, annual job fairs, and career counseling services before graduation.

Review and analyze a job requisition booklet before you enter the labor market. Remember that it is your responsibility to contact the placement counselors at your school, so that they may assist in your career development program.

SOLUTIONS

Multiple Choice:	True/False:	Matching:
1. a	1. False	1. b
2. b	2. False	2. i
3. c	3. False	3. o
4. d	4. True	4. a
5. a	5. False	5. e
6. b	6. False	6. g
7. a	7. False	7. m
8. c	8. True	8. q
9. d	9. True	9. l
10. c	10. False	10. f
11. b	11. False	11. k
12. a	12. True	12. r
13. d	13. False	13. s
14. a	14. False	14. h
15. c	15. False	15. n
16. b	16. False	16. c
17. d	17. True	17. p
18. d	18. True	18. d
19. c	19. True	19. j
20. a	20. False	20. t
21. c	21. True	21. u
22. b	22. True	22. v
23. d	23. False	
24. a	24. False	
25. a	25. True	
26. c		
27. c		
28. c		
29. a		
30. b		

False Statements Made True

1. Dramatic shifts in the composition of the labor force require managers to become **more** involved in planning.

2. The **mission** is the basic purpose of the organization, as well as its scope of operations.
3. Although the terms *mission* and *vision* are often used interchangeably, the **vision** statement ideally clarifies the long-term direction of the company and its strategic intent.
5. One of the most important assessments a firm can make is identifying the needs of its **customers**.
6. At times, the biggest opportunity or threat in an industry **does not** come from direct competition, **but from substitution**.
7. According to the U.S. Census Bureau, employment growth will continue to be concentrated in the **service-providing** sector.
10. In many cases, **people** are a key resource that underlies a firm's core capabilities.
11. People are a source of competitive advantage when employee capabilities and contributions **cannot** be copied by others.
13. **Core employees** have skills that are quite valuable to a company, but not particularly unique.
14. Ideally forecasting should include **both quantitative and qualitative** methods.
15. Forecasting is frequently more an **art** than a **science**.
16. Qualitative approaches to forecasting are **less** statistical than quantitative approaches.
20. Some estimates suggest that only about **15 percent** of all mergers achieve their objectives (measured by return on investment, shareholder value, and the like).
23. The target company for benchmarking **does not** need to be a competitor.
24. **Coordination** flexibility occurs through rapid reallocation of resources to new or changing needs.

PART TWO

Meeting Human Resources Requirements

CHAPTER

3

EQUAL EMPLOYMENT OPPORTUNITY AND HUMAN RESOURCES MANAGEMENT

In this chapter you will learn how managers must be constantly aware of the laws and regulations governing the employment relationship. This is true for both federal and state regulations. Many of these laws concern the fair and equal employment of protected classes of workers, although equal employment opportunity (EEO) laws pertain to all members of the labor force. You will understand from this chapter that equal employment opportunity laws cover all aspects of employment, including recruitment, selection, training, promotion, and compensation. In hiring or supervising employees, you will know to give careful attention to the application of equal employment opportunity laws and regulations to prevent charges of discrimination. Finally, you will be able to distinguish how protected classes can sustain a charge of adverse impact, how an employer can establish a defense of adverse impact, and how the employer should establish an affirmative action program.

LEARNING OBJECTIVES

After studying this chapter, you should be able to

1. Explain the reasons behind passage of EEO legislation.
2. Prepare an outline describing the major laws affecting equal employment opportunity, and describe bona fide occupational qualification and religious preference as EEO issues.
3. Discuss sexual harassment and immigration reform and control as EEO concerns.
4. Explain the use of the *Uniform Guidelines on Employee Selection Procedures.*
5. Understand the concepts of adverse impact and disparate treatment.
6. Understand EEOC recordkeeping and posting requirements.

7 Understand how EEO discrimination charges are processed.

8 Describe affirmative action and the basic steps in developing an affirmative action program.

CHAPTER SUMMARY RELATING TO LEARNING OBJECTIVES

1 Employment discrimination against blacks, Hispanics, women, and other groups. has long been practiced by US employers. Prejudice against minority groups is a major cause in their lack of employment gains. Government reports show that the wages and job opportunities of minorities typically lag behind those for whites.

2 Effective management requires knowing the legal aspects of the employment relationship. Pertinent legislation includes the Equal Pay Act, Title VII of the Civil Rights Act of 1964, the Age Discrimination in Employment Act, the Equal Employment Opportunity Act of 1972, the Pregnancy Discrimination Act, the Americans with Disabilities Act, the Civil Rights Act of 1991, and various executive orders. Employers are permitted to discriminate against selected protected classes where hiring preferences are a reasonable necessity, constituting a bona fide occupational qualification for normal business operation. The religious preference of employees must be accommodated as required by law.

3 Sexual harassment is an area of particular importance for managers and supervisors. Extensive efforts should be made to ensure that both male and female employees are free from all forms of sexually harassing conduct. The Immigration Reform and Control Act was passed to control unauthorized immigration into United States. The law requires managers to maintain various employment records, and they must not discriminate against job applicants or present employees because of national origin or citizenship status.

4 The *Uniform Guidelines on Employee Selection Procedures* is designed to help employers comply with federal prohibitions against employment practices that discriminate on the basis of race, color, religion, gender, or national origin. The *Uniform Guidelines* provide employers with a framework for making legally enforceable employment decisions. Employers must be able to show that selection procedures are valid in predicting job performance.

5 Adverse impact plays an important role in proving employment discrimination. Adverse impact means that an employer's employment practices result in the rejection of a significantly higher percentage of members of minority and other protected groups for some employment activity. A key to an adverse impact discrimination claim is that the employer's employment practice is unintentional in its impact against the protected group. Disparate treatment is intentional discrimination against the protected group. Refusing to hire individuals of a particular religion or denying males, but not females, office clerical jobs are examples of disparate treatment.

6 To ensure that organizations comply with antidiscrimination legislation, the EEOC was established to monitor employers' actions. Employers subject to federal laws must maintain required records and report requested employment statistics when mandated. Employers with 100 or more employees must file an EEO-1 report annually. This comprehensive document identifies employees by race/ethnicity and gender for 10 job categories. Companies with government contracts of $50,000 or more must file an affirmative action plan with the OFCCP. Employers are required to collect employment data and file reports under various federal and state laws. Employers are also required to post EEO posters and posters for other government programs in prominent locations.

7 Employees or applicants for employment who believe they have been discriminated against file a discrimination complaint (a charge form) with the EEOC. The employer receives a copy of the charge form which initiates an EEOC investigation of the alleged discrimination. Individual claiming discrimination must file the complaint within 180 days of the alleged offense, 300 days in deferral states. After the investigation, the Commission may dismiss the charge. The paintiff will receive a right-to-sue notice which allows the individual to start private litigation. If the EEOC finds reasonable cause for the charge, it will attempt to mediate a settlement between the parties. If an agreement is not reached, the EEOC may elect to sue the employer in federal court. Figure 3.5 illustrates the steps in filing a discrimination charge.

8 Affirmative action goes beyond providing equal employment opportunity to employees. Affirmative action requires employers to become proactive and correct areas of past discrimination. This is accomplished by employing protected classes for jobs where they are underrepresented. The employer's goal is to have a balanced internal workforce representative of the employer's relevant labor market.

REVIEW QUESTIONS

Multiple Choice

Choose the letter of the word or phrase that best completes each statement.

1

_______ 1. The treatment of individuals in all aspects of employment, hiring, promotion, training, etc., in a fair and nonbiased manner is
a. equal employment opportunity.
b. sexual harassment.
c. age discrimination.
d. the four-fifths rule.

1

_______ 2. A central aim of political action has been to establish justice for all people of the nation through the protection of the
a. United States Constitution.
b. Fair Labor Standards.
c. Equal Pay Act.
d. Uniform Commercial Partnership Act.

2

_______ 3. Major federal EEO laws have attempted to correct social problems of interest to particular groups of workers called
a. affirmative action.
b. knowledge workers.
c. protected classes.
d. bona fide occupational qualification.

2

_______ 4. The act that outlaws discrimination in pay, employee benefits, and pensions based on the worker's gender is the
a. Equal Employment Opportunity Act.
b. Equal Pay Act.
c. Age Discrimination in Employment Act.
d. Americans with Disabilities Act.

2

_______ 5. The Equal Pay Act was passed as an amendment to the
a. Equal Employment Opportunity Act.
b. Equal Pay Act.
c. Age Discrimination in Employment Act.
d. Fair Labor Standards Act

2 _______ 6. The Civil Rights Act of 1964 and the Civil Rights Act of 1991 cover a broad range of organizations, *except*
a. all private employers in interstate commerce who employ fifteen or more employees.
b. all foreign organizations doing business in their domestic countries.
c. state and local governments.
d. private and public employment agencies, including the U.S. Employment Service.

2 _______ 7. Under Title VII of the Civil Rights Act, employers are permitted limited exemptions from antidiscrimination employment preferences based on a
a. commercial code.
b. past practice.
c. common law.
d. bona fide occupational qualification.

2 _______ 8. A practice that is necessary for the safe and efficient operation of the organization, as interpreted by the courts, is a defense based on
a. religious preference.
b. self-defense.
c. business necessity.
d. age discrimination.

2 _______ 9. The Pregnancy Discrimination Act affects employees' benefit programs in the following areas, *except*
a. hospital and major medical insurance.
b. vacation and holiday pay.
c. temporary disability and salary continuation plans.
d. sick leave policies.

2 _______ 10. Discrimination against the disabled was first prohibited in federally funded activities by the
a. The Pregnancy Discrimination Act
b. Vocational Rehabilitation Act
c. Americans with Disabilities Act
d. Civil Rights Act

2

_______ 11. In *Toyota v Williams,* the Supreme Court ruled that if a physical or mental impairment is correctable, then it is not a
a. competitive reaction.
b. disability.
c. mental impairment.
d. physical disease.

2

_______ 12. An attempt by employers to adjust, without undue hardship, the working conditions or schedules of employees with disabilities or religious preferences is based on
a. reasonable accommodation.
b. labor contracts.
c. fairness and inequities.
d. job analysis.

3

_______ 13. Unwelcome advances, requests for sexual favors, and other verbal or physical conduct of a sexual nature constitutes
a. fraud.
b. antidiscrimination.
c. sexual harassment.
d. misrepresentation of fact.

3

_______ 14. Illegal __________ has/have adversely affected welfare services and educational and Social Security benefits in the United States.
a. protected classes
b. immigration
c. uniform guidelines
d. bona fide occupational qualifications

4

_______ 15. An important procedural document for managers that applies to employee selection procedures in the areas of hiring, retention, promotion, transfer, demotion, dismissal, and referral is
a. affirmative action.
b. employee leasing.
c. *Uniform Guidelines.*
d. sexual harassment rules.

4

_______ 16. When using a test or other selection instrument to choose individuals for employment, employers must be able to prove
a. affirmative action.
b. adverse impact.
c. disparate treatment.
d. validity.

5 _______ 17. For an applicant or employee to pursue a discrimination case successfully, the individual must establish that the employer's selection procedures resulted in a(n)
a. adverse impact on a protected class.
b. undue process.
c. affirmative action claim.
d. violation of human rights.

5 _______ 18. As a rule of thumb to determine adverse impact on enforcement proceedings, the Equal Employment Opportunity Commission has adopted
a. affirmative action procedures.
b. the four-fifths rule.
c. minimal wage provisions.
d. overtime provisions.

5 _______ 19. The act of purposeful discrimination by an employer is called
a. disparate treatment.
b. adverse impact.
c. antidiscrimination.
d. bona fide occupational qualifications.

5 _______ 20. *Griggs v Duke Power Co.* was concerned with a minority person meeting the qualifications for a position as a coal handler and exposed problems with
a. sexual harassment.
b. employment selection procedures.
c. job burnout.
d. employment fatigue.

5 _______ 21. The type of analysis that will classify protected-class members by number and the type of job they hold within the organization is
a. adverse impact.
b. workforce utilization.
c. business necessity.
d. adverse treatment.

5 _______ 22. A benchmark case in which the Supreme Court established two important principles—that discrimination need not be overt or intentional and that employment practices must be job-related—was
a. *Hopwood v State of Texas.*

b. *Albermarle Paper Company v Moody.*
c. *Wards Cove Packing Company v Antonio.*
d. *Griggs v Duke Power Company.*

5 _______ 23. The commission that was created from Title VII of the Civil Rights Act of 1964 was the
a. Security Exchange Commission.
b. Federal Trade Commission.
c. Equal Employment Opportunity Commission.
d. Business Necessity Commission.

6 _______ 24. Employers of 100 or more employees (except state and local government employers) and government contractors and subcontractors subject to Executive Order 11286 must file annually a(n)
a. Business Office Report.
b. Human Resources Plan.
c. Labor Office Hours Report.
d. EEO-1 report (Employer Information Report).

8 _______ 25. A policy that goes beyond equal employment opportunity by requiring organizations to comply with the law and correct past discriminatory practices by increasing the numbers of minorities and women in specific positions is
a. human resources planning.
b. job evaluation.
c. performance appraisal.
d. affirmative action.

8 _______ 26. The following are reasons employers establish affirmative action programs, *except*
a. provide an organizational profile that graphically illustrates their workforce demographics.
b. establishing goals and timetables for employment of underutilized protected classes.
c. monitor progress of the entire affirmative action program.
d. develop a reactive strategy for recruitment and selection.

8 _______ 27. The act of giving preference to members of protected classes to the extent that unprotected individuals believe they are suffering discrimination is
a. reverse discrimination.
b. job analysis.
c. job evaluation.
d. performance appraisal.

8 _______ 28. One of the most famous reverse discrimination cases is
a. *Griggs v Duke Power Company.*
b. *Regents of the University of California v Bakke.*
c. *Wards Cove Packing Company v Antonio.*
d. *Hopwood v State of Texas.*

8 _______ 29. Equal employment opportunity legislation requires managers to provide the same opportunities to
a. customers and suppliers.
b. all job applicants and employees regardless of ethnicity.
c. business agents and labor unions.
d. government agents and officials.

8 _______ 30. In *Grutter v Bollinger*, the Supreme Court held that colleges and universities can consider as a factor in admission decisions, an applicant's
a. race.
b. height.
c. weight.
d. name.

True/False

Identify the following statements as True or False.

1 _______ 1. Equal employment opportunity is a legal topic, however, it is not an emotional issue.

1 _______ 2. Equal employment opportunity as a national priority has emerged slowly in the United States.

1 _______ 3. The change in government and societal attitudes toward discrimination was further prompted by decreasing public awareness of the economic imbalance between nonwhites and whites.

1 _______ 4. Since as early as the nineteenth century, the public has not been informed or aware of discriminatory employment practices in the United States.

2 _______ 5. Laws have been passed barring discrimination pertaining to recruitment, selection, performance appraisal, promotion, and compensation.

2 _______ 6. Employers violate the Equal Pay Act when differences in wages paid to men and women for equal work are based on seniority systems, merit considerations, or incentive pay plans.

2 _______ 7. Employers may defend their employment practices by a defense of bona fide occupational qualifications and/or business necessity.

2 _______ 8. Title VII of the Civil Rights Act of 1991 requires employers to grant complete religious freedom in employment situations.

2 _______ 9. The chances of age discrimination by employers are expected to increase over time.

2 _______ 10. Fair employment practices are state and local laws governing equal employment opportunity that are often less comprehensive than federal laws.

3 _______ 11. Quid pro quo sexual harassment can occur when unwelcome sexual conduct has the purpose or effect of unreasonably interfering with job performance.

3 _______ 12. In a hostile environment, sexual harassment can occur when submission to or rejection of sexual conduct is used as a basis for employment decisions.

4 _______ 13. Employers are completely certain about the appropriateness of specific selection procedures, especially those related to testing and selection.

4 _______ 14. Under the *Uniform Guidelines*, the use of any selection procedure that has an adverse impact on the hiring, promotion, or other employment or membership opportunities of members of any race, sex, or ethnic group is considered to be discriminatory.

5 ______ 15. Adverse impact refers to the rejection for employment, placement, or promotion of a significantly lower percentage of a nonprotected class when compared with a protected class.

5 ______ 16. An alternative to the population comparison rule, and one increasingly used in discrimination lawsuits, is to apply the 80/20 analysis to the observed applicant flow data.

5 ______ 17. Hiring individuals who must meet a minimum height or appearance standard (at the expense of protected class members) is evidence of a restricted policy by an employer.

5 ______ 18. The *Uniform Guidelines* have been given added importance through three leading Supreme Court cases; each case is noteworthy because it elaborates on the concepts of affirmative action, job enlargement, and job enrichment.

5 ______ 19. Equal Employment Opportunity Commission guidelines are not federal mandates by administrative rules and regulations published in the *Federal Register*.

5 ______ 20. Equal Employment Opportunity Commission investigations are conducted by fully trained equal opportunity specialists (EOSs) who have extensive experience in investigative procedures, theories of discrimination, and relief and remedy techniques.

7 ______ 21. Managers and supervisors must retaliate against individuals who invoke their legal rights to file charges or to support other employees during Equal Employment Opportunity Commission proceedings.

7 ______ 22. Since managers and supervisors are key to preventing and correcting discrimination, they, in particular, must be trained to understand employee rights and managerial obligations.

8 ______ 23. Affirmative action is achieved by having organizations follow specific guidelines and establish goals to ensure that they have a balanced and representative workforce.

8 ______ 24. Affirmative action has consistently resulted in improvement of the employment status of protected groups.

8

_______ 25. Since the beginning of the 1990s, federal courts have decreasingly restricted the use of race and ethnicity in awarding scholarships, determining college admissions, making layoff decisions, selecting employees, promoting employees, and awarding government contracts.

Matching

Match each term with the proper definition.

Terms

a. adverse impact
b. affirmative action
c. bona fide occupational qualification (BFOQ)
d. business necessity
e. charge form
f. disabled individual
g. disparate treatment
h. EEO-1 report
i. equal employment opportunity
j. fair employment practices (FEPs)
k. four-fifths rule
l. protected classes
m. reasonable accommodation
n. reverse discrimination
o. sexual harassment
p. *Uniform Guidelines on Employee Selection Procedures*
q. workforce utilization analysis

Definitions

_______ 1. any person who has a physical or mental impairment that substantially limits such person's major life activities

_______ 2. act of giving preference to members of protected classes to the extent that unprotected individuals believe they are suffering discrimination

_______ 3. the treatment of individuals in all aspects of employment—hiring, promotion, training, etc.— in a fair and nonbiased manner

_______ 4. individuals of a minority race, women, older persons, and those with disabilities who are covered by federal laws on equal employment opportunity

_______ 5. attempt by employers to adjust, without undue hardship, the working conditions or schedules of employees with disabilities or religious preferences

_______ 6. state and local laws governing equal employment opportunity that are often more comprehensive than federal laws

_______ 7. procedural document published in the *Federal Register* to assist employers in complying with federal regulations against discriminatory actions

_______ 8. a concept that refers to the rejection of a significantly higher percentage of a protected class for employment, placement, or promotion when compared with the successful, nonprotected class

_______ 9. rule of thumb followed by the Equal Employment Opportunity Commission in determining adverse impact in enforcement proceedings

_______ 10. process of classifying protected class members by number and by the type of job they hold within the organization

_______ 11. situation in which protected-class members receive unequal treatment or are evaluated by different standards

_______ 12. unwelcome advances, requests for sexual favors, and other verbal or physical conduct of a sexual nature in the working environment

_______ 13. suitable defense against a discrimination charge only where age, religion, sex, or national origin is an actual qualification for performing the job

_______ 14. work-related practice that is necessary for the safe and efficient operation of an organization

_______ 15. an employer information report that must be filed annually by employers of 100 or more employees (except state and local government employers) and government contractors and subcontractors to determine an employer's workforce composition

_______ 16. discrimination complaint filed with the Equal Employment Opportunity Commission by employees or job applicants

_______ 17. policy that goes beyond equal employment opportunity by requiring organizations to comply with the law and to correct past discriminatory practices by increasing the numbers of minorities and women in specific positions

Internet Exercises

Examine the implications of the Supreme Court Decision in Smith v. City of Jackson for ADEA.
http://digitalcommons.ilr.cornell.edu/cgi/viewcontent.cgi?article=1184&context=key_workplace

Why is workplace diversity prized in the business community?
http://www.findarticles.com/p/articles/mi_m3495/is_9_48/ai_108315218/print.

How to Proceed with a Charge of Discrimination against an Employer

Assume you are a minority student from a protected class. How could you charge an employer with discrimination if you are a candidate and are denied employment for a job that has been advertised?

An individual may take a discrimination charge against an employer to the regional office of the Equal Employment Opportunity Commission or take the charge to the state Human Relations Commission.

An individual can bring forth a charge of adverse impact against an employer. This concept refers to the rejection of a significantly higher percentage of a protected class for employment, placement, or promotion when compared with the successful nonprotected class of individuals. An individual can charge an employer with disparate treatment, which is a situation in which protected-class members receive unequal treatment or are evaluated by different standards.

Individuals can bring forth a charge of the violation of the four-fifths rule against an employer, which is a rule of thumb followed by the Equal Employment Opportunity Commission in determining adverse impact for use in enforcement proceedings.

Any evidence that an employer has a selection procedure that excludes members of a protected class, whether intentional or not, constitutes adverse impact. Hiring individuals who must meet a minimum height or appearance standard (at the expense of protected class members) is evidence of such a restrictive policy.

Individuals who believe they have been unjustly rejected for employment may demonstrate disparate treatment through the McDonnell Douglas test.

SOLUTIONS

Multiple Choice:

1. a
2. a
3. c
4. b

True/False:

1. False
2. True
3. False
4. False

Matching:

1. f
2. n
3. i
4. l

5. d
6. b
7. d
8. c
9. b
10. b
11. b
12. a
13. c
14. b
15. c
16. d
17. a
18. b
19. a
20. b
21. b
22. d
23. c
24. d
25. d
26. d
27. a
28. b
29. b
30. a

5. True
6. False
7. True
8. False
9. True
10. False
11. False
12. False
13. False
14. True
15. False
16. False
17. True
18. False
19. False
20. True
21. False
22. True
23. True
24. False
25. False

5. m
6. j
7. p
8. a
9. k
10. q
11. g
12. o
13. c
14. d
15. h
16. e
17. b

False Statements Made True

1. Equal employment opportunity is **not only** a legal topic **but also an emotional issue**.
3. The change in government and societal attitudes toward discrimination was further prompted by **increasing** public awareness of the economic imbalance between nonwhites and whites.
4. Since as early as the nineteenth century, **the public has been aware** of discriminatory employment practices in the United States.
6. Employers **do not violate** the Equal Pay Act when differences in wages paid to men and women for equal work are based on seniority systems, merit considerations, or incentive pay plans.
8. Title VII of the Civil Rights Act of 1964 **does not** require employers to grant complete religious freedom in employment situations.

10. Fair employment practices are state and local laws governing equal employment opportunity that are often **more** comprehensive than federal laws.
11. Quid pro quo sexual harassment can occur when **submission to or rejection of sexual conduct is used as a basis for employment decisions.**
12. In a hostile environment, sexual harassment can occur when **unwelcome sexual conduct has the purpose or effect of unreasonably interfering with job performance or creating an intimidating, hostile, or offensive working environment.**
13. Employers are **often uncertain** about the appropriateness of specific selection procedures, especially those related to testing and selection.
15. Adverse impact refers to the rejection for employment, placement, or promotion of a significantly **higher** percentage of a **protected class** when compared with a **nonprotected class**.
16. An alternative to **the four-fifths rule**, and one increasingly used in discrimination lawsuits, is to apply the ***standard deviation analysis*** to the observed applicant flow data.
18. The *Uniform Guidelines* have been given added importance through three leading Supreme Court cases; each case is noteworthy because it elaborates on the concepts of **adverse impact, validity testing, and job relatedness**.
19. Equal Employment Opportunity Commission guidelines are not federal law **but administrative rules and regulations published in the *Federal Register*.**
21. Managers and supervisors **must not** retaliate against individuals who invoke their legal rights to file charges or to support other employees during Equal Employment Opportunity Commission proceedings.
24. Affirmative action **has not** consistently resulted in improvement of the employment status of protected groups.
25. **Since the mid-1990s**, federal courts have **increasingly** restricted the use of race and ethnicity in awarding scholarships, determining college admissions, making layoff decisions, selecting employees, promoting employees, and awarding government contracts.

CHAPTER

4

JOB ANALYSIS, EMPLOYEE INVOLVEMENT, AND FLEXIBLE WORK SCHEDULES

In this chapter you will learn the relationship between job requirements and the performance of human resources management functions. You will learn that job requirements provide the foundation on which many human resources decisions, including those relating to recruitment, selection, training, evaluation, and compensation, must be based. It is essential that the requirements of each job in the organization are determined accurately. Supervisors and their employees must be aware of these job requirements. You will learn the relevance of job analysis and how it is used to write job descriptions and job specifications.

You will also understand the techniques used to maximize employee contributions, be able to discuss the various job characteristics that motivate employees, and, finally, explain how managers can implement alternative work schedules.

LEARNING OBJECTIVES

After studying this chapter, you should be able to

1. Discuss the relationship between job requirements and the performance of HRM functions.

2. Indicate the methods by which job analysis typically is completed.

3. Identify and explain the various sections of job descriptions.

4. Provide examples illustrating the various factors that must be taken into account in designing a job.

5. Discuss the various job characteristics that motivate employees.

6. Describe the different group techniques used to maximize employee contributions.

7. Differentiate and explain the different adjustments in work schedules.

CHAPTER SUMMARY RELATING TO LEARNING OBJECTIVES

1 Job requirements reflect the different duties, tasks, and responsibilities contained in jobs. Job requirements, in turn, influence the human resources function performed by managers, including recruitment, selection, training and development, performance appraisal, compensation, and various labor relations activities.

2 Job analysis data may be gathered using several collection methods: interviews, questionnaires, observations, and diaries. Other, more quantitative approaches include the position analysis questionnaire system, critical incident method, task inventory analysis, and competency-based job analysis. It is the prevailing opinion of the courts that human resources management decisions on employment, performance appraisal, and promotions must be based on specific criteria that are job-related. These criteria can be determined objectively only by analyzing the requirements of each job.

3 The format of job descriptions varies widely, often reflecting the needs of the organization and the expertise of the writer. As a minimum, job descriptions should contain a job title, a job identification section, and an essential function section. A job specification section also may be included. Job descriptions should be written in clear and specific terms with consideration given to their legal implications.

4 Job design is a combination of four basic considerations: organizational objectives; industrial engineering concerns of analyzing work methods and establishing time standards; ergonomic considerations, which accommodate human capabilities and limitations to job tasks; and employee contributions.

5 In the job characteristics model, five job factors contribute to increased job performance and satisfaction: skill task variety, task identity, task significance, autonomy, and feedback. All factors should be built into jobs since each factor influences different employee psychological states. When jobs are enriched in the job characteristics model, employees experience more meaningfulness in their jobs, they acquire more job responsibility, and they receive direct feedback from the tasks they perform.

6 To improve the internal process of organizations and increase American productivity, greater efforts are made by organizations to involve group of employees in work operations. Employee involvement groups are composed of employees in work units charged with offering suggestions for improving product or service quality or fostering workplace effectiveness. Employee teams stress employee collaboration over individual accomplishment. Teams rely on the expertise and different abilities of members to achieve a specific goal or objective. Self-directed teams are characterized by their willingness to perform traditional managerial tasks.

7 Changes in work schedules which include the compressed workweek, flextime, job sharing, and telecommuting permit employees to adjust their work periods to accommodate their particular lifestyles. Employees can select from among these human resources techniques to accommodate diverse employee needs while fostering organizational effectiveness.

REVIEW QUESTIONS

Multiple Choice

Choose the letter of the word or phrase that best completes each statement.

1 ________ 1. A group of related activities and duties is a
   a. job.
   b. position.
   c. salary range.
   d. pay grade.

1 ________ 2. The different duties and responsibilities performed by a single employee make up a
   a. job.
   b. position.
   c. salary range.
   d. pay grade.

1 ________ 3. The purposes of recruitment, training, compensation, or advancement opportunities may be grouped into a
   a. position description.
   b. job enlargement.
   c. job analysis.
   d. job family.

1 ________ 4. Before capable employees can be found for an organization, recruiters need to know the
a. critical incident method.
b. job specifications.
c. job analysis method.
d. participant diary log.

1 ________ 5. Job specifications establish the qualifications required of applicants and play an essential role in the
a. recruiting function.
b. functional job analysis.
c. job characteristics model.
d. production function.

1 ________ 6. A statement of the tasks, duties, and responsibilities of a job is a
a. job family.
b. job specification.
c. job description.
d. position.

2 ________ 7. Human resources managers use job analysis data to develop
a. attitude and behavior surveys.
b. job descriptions and job specifications.
c. functional job analysis and ergonomics issues.
d. employee and labor union contracts.

2 ________ 8. Accurate job data must be collected from employees in order to create an effective
a. affirmative action program.
b. job analysis.
c. employer association.
d. quota system.

2 ________ 9. The job analysis technique that is worker-oriented and covers 194 different tasks is
a. task inventory development.
b. the critical incident method.
c. functional job analysis.
d. the position analysis questionnaire.

2 _______ 10. The job analysis technique that was pioneered by the US Air Force is
a. task inventory development.
b. the critical incident method.
c. functional job analysis.
d. the position analysis questionnaire.

2 _______ 11. The job analysis technique that relies on building job profiles that look at the responsibility and activities of jobs and the worker competencies necessary to accomplish them is
a. task inventory development.
b. the critical incident method.
c. the competency-based analysis.
d. the position analysis questionnaire.

3 _______ 12. Most job descriptions contain all of the following *except*
a. job title.
b. job identification.
c. job duties section.
d. job evaluation section.

3 _______ 13. From the employer's standpoint, written ________ can minimize the misunderstandings that occur between managers and their subordinates concerning job requirements.
a. job specifications
b. position analysis questionnaires
c. job descriptions
d. critical incidences

3 _______ 14. The section of a job description that provides information about the location of the job and the reporting relationships involved is the
a. job identification section.
b. job duty section.
c. job title.
d. job specification.

4 _______ 15. The term that describes the process that is concerned with structuring jobs in order to improve the organization's efficiency and employee satisfaction is
a. job specification.

b. job analysis.
c. job design.
d. job selection.

4 _______ 16. In order to capture the talents of employees while improving organization performance, job design is concerned with
a. modifying jobs.
b. changing jobs.
c. enriching jobs.
d. all of the above.

4 _______ 17. What consideration of job design includes worker' physical and mental capabilities?
a. Organizational objectives
b. Industrial engineering concerns
c. Ergonomic considerations
d. Behavioral concerns

4 _______ 18. Any effort that makes work more rewarding or satisfying by adding more meaningful tasks to an employee's job is
a. job enlargement.
b. job specification.
c. job enrichment.
d. job analysis.

4 _______ 19. Herzberg's concept of fulfilling employee needs such as self-fulfillment and self-esteem while achieving long-term job satisfaction and performance goals is known as
a. job enlargement.
b. job specification.
c. job enrichment.
d. job analysis.

5 _______ 20. The following are traits in the job characteristics model *except*
a. skill variety.
b. task identity.
c. task significance.
d. consensus decision making.

5 ______ 21. A technique of involving employees in their work through the process of inclusion is
a. employee empowerment.
b. employee downsizing.
c. job enlargement.
d. reengineering of work.

5 ______ 22. The process that attempts to accommodate the human capabilities and limitations of those who are to perform a job is
a. job analysis.
b. job enrichment.
c. ergonomics.
d. job enlargement.

5 ______ 23. The field of study that is concerned with analyzing work methods and establishing time standards is
a. job analysis.
b. job enrichment.
c. ergonomics.
d. Industrial engineering

6 ______ 24. Those participating in employee involvement groups (EIs) must receive comprehensive training in problem identification, problem analysis, and various decision-making tools such as
a. program and nonprogram decisions.
b. quality circles and self-managed teams.
c. centralized and decentralized authority.
d. statistical analysis and cause-and-effect diagrams.

6 ______ 25. A logical outgrowth of employment involvement work groups and the philosophy of employee empowerment would be
a. labor unions.
b. informal groups of employees.
c. employee teams.
d. temporary work groups.

6 ______ 26. Advanced computer and telecommunications technology to link team members who are geographically dispersed, often worldwide, are
a. employee involvement groups.
b. virtual teams.

c. job analysis.
d. flextime workers.

7 _______ 27. From the employer's standpoint, flextime can be most helpful in
a. predicting employee turnover.
b. recruiting and retaining personnel.
c. developing job sharing.
d. flexible and adaptable work schedules.

7 _______ 28. The arrangement whereby two part-time employees perform a job that otherwise would be held by one full-time employee is called
a. job sharing.
b. job rotation.
c. flextime.
d. flexible schedules.

7 _______ 29. The following are disadvantages to flextime *except*
a. It improves service to customers/clients by extending operating hours.
b. It is not suited for some jobs.
c. It creates communications problems for managers and employees.
d. Managers may have to extend their workweek.

7 _______ 30. Use of personal computers and communication technology to do work at home that is traditionally done in the workplace is called
a. job sharing.
b. job rotation.
c. flextime.
d. telecommuting

True/False

Identify the following statements as True or False.

1 _______ 1. Any discrepancies between the knowledge, skills, and abilities demonstrated by a jobholder and the requirements contained in the description and specification for that job provide clues to training needs.

1 _______ 2. The requirements contained in the description of a job provide the criteria for evaluating the performance of the holder of that job.

1 _______ 3. In determining the rate to be paid for performing a job, the relative worth of the job would be the least important factor to be considered.

2 _______ 4. Job analysis is the process of obtaining information about jobs by determining what the duties, tasks, or activities of those jobs are.

2 _______ 5. The job descriptions and job specifications developed through job analysis should be as inaccurate as possible if they are to be of value to those who make human resources management (HRM) decisions.

2 _______ 6. Common methods of analyzing jobs when undertaking job analysis would include interviews, questionnaires, observation, and diaries.

2 _______ 7. The task inventory method can be considered a job-oriented type of job analysis.

2 _______ 8. The objective of the critical incident method of job analysis is to identify 194 items in the checklist of the position analysis questionnaire.

3 _______ 9. In writing a job description, selection of a job title is important in providing status to the employee; for example, "sanitation engineer" is preferable to "garbage collector."

3 _______ 10. Skills that are irrelevant to a job include education, social interaction, specialized training, personal traits or abilities, and family dexterities.

3 _______ 11. When writing a job description, it is essential to use statements that are loose, vague, and comprehensive.

4 _______ 12. There are two job design methods—job enrichment and job characteristics—which seek to incorporate the behavioral needs of employees as they perform their individual jobs.

4 _______ 13. Job enlargement, or the vertical expansion of jobs, may be accomplished by increasing the autonomy and responsibility of employees.

5 _______ 14. According to Richard Hackman and Greg Oldham, their job characteristics model proposes that three psychological states of a jobholder result in improved work performance, internal motivation, and lower absenteeism and turnover.

5 _______ 15. Empowerment encourages employees to become innovators and managers of their own work, and it involves them in their jobs in ways that give them more control and autonomous decision-making capabilities.

5 _______ 16. The outgrowth of scientific management was industrial engineering, which is concerned with analyzing work methods and establishing time standards.

5 _______ 17. Ergonomics is concerned with equipment design and must only take into consideration the mental ability of operators to use the equipment and to react through vision, hearing, and touch to the information the equipment conveys.

5 _______ 18. Ergonomics has recently focused on the increase and inclusion of many repetitive motion injuries, particularly those related to the back and wrist.

6 _______ 19. Designing work to enhance group or worker productivity includes the techniques of collaboration and synergy.

6 _______ 20. Permanent groups of five to ten employees doing similar or related work who meet together regularly to identify, analyze, and suggest solutions to shared problems are often referred to as task forces.

6 _______ 21. Job enrichment occurs when the interactions and outcomes of team members are greater than the sum of their individual efforts.

6 _______ 22. Work teams can operate in a variety of organization structures, each with different strategic purposes or functional activities.

7 _______ 23. Flextime, or flexible working hours, permits employees the option of choosing daily starting and quitting times, provided they work a certain number of hours per day or week.

7 _______ 24. Telecommuting is the use of personal computers, networks, and other communications technology such as fax machines to do work in the home that is traditionally done in the workplace.

7 _______ 25. A variant of telecommuting is the cyber workspace where employees are in the office selling to, or servicing, customers or are stationed at other remote locations working as if they were in the field.

Matching

Match each term with the proper definition.

Terms

a. critical incident method
b. employee empowerment
c. employee involvement groups (EIs)
d. employee teams
e. ergonomics
f. flextime
g. virtual team
h. industrial engineering
i. job
j. job analysis
k. job characteristics model
l. job description
m. job design
n. job enrichment
o. job family
p. job specification
q. position
r. position analysis questionnaire (PAQ)
s. task inventory analysis
t. telecommuting

Definitions

_______ 1. flexible working hours that give employees the option of choosing daily starting and quitting times, provided that they work a set number of hours per day or week

_______ 2. empowerment approach that purports that improving the psychological state of a jobholder results in improved work performance, internal motivation, and lower absenteeism and turnover

_______ 3. statement of the needed knowledge, skills, and abilities of the person who is to perform the job

_______ 4. different jobs that have similar duties and responsibilities

_______ 5. granting employees power to initiate change, thereby encouraging them to take charge of what they do

_______ 6. use of personal computers, networks, and other communications technology to do work in the home that has traditionally been done in the workplace

_______ 7. outgrowth of job analysis that improves jobs and is concerned with structuring jobs in order to improve organization efficiency and employee job satisfaction

_______ 8. a field of study concerned with analyzing work methods and establishing time standards

_______ 9. logical outgrowth of employee involvement and the philosophy of empowerment

_______ 10. an interdisciplinary approach to designing equipment and systems that can be easily and efficiently used by employees

_______ 11. the different duties and responsibilities performed by a single employee

_______ 12. job analysis method in which important job tasks are identified for job success

_______ 13. process of obtaining information about a job by determining the job's duties, tasks, or activities

_______ 14. enhancing a job by adding more meaningful tasks and duties to make the work more rewarding or satisfying

_______ 15. a team with widely dispersed members linked through computer and telecommunications technology

_______ 16. questionnaire covering 194 different tasks which, by means of a five-point scale, seeks to determine the degree to which different tasks are involved in performing a particular job

_______ 17. a group of related activities and duties

_______ 18. groups of employees who meet to resolve problems or offer suggestions for organizational improvement

_______ 19. statement of a job's tasks, duties, and responsibilities

_______ 20. an organized list of tasks and their descriptions used as a basis to identify components of different jobs

Internet Exercises

What alternative work arrangements are used by an employer?
http://careerplanning.about.com/cs/flextime/a/flextime.htm.

How is job analysis used as an employment tool?
http://www.ucp.org/ucp_channeldoc.cfm/1/17/11928/11928-11928/4605

How to Request a Realistic Job Preview

A job applicant may request a realistic job preview when interviewing with an employer or the Human Resources Department.

A line manager or the Human Resources Department should provide a realistic job preview in every interview. This process is an accurate portrayal of the job that the applicant is expected to perform. It would include the job title, duties and responsibilities, and the authority delegated in the performance of a job. Opportunities for growth and a career development program should be discussed to provide the greatest amount of information to each job applicant. Remember, it is the responsibility of the individual applying for a job or the employee to initiate the discussion of a career development program. One can also ask to see a job specification, which outlines the minimal qualifications required for a job. A job specification specifies the abilities and skills required to perform a job. It includes the educational requirements and work experiences necessary. An applicant should attempt to match these job requirements to his or her own strengths.

SOLUTIONS

Multiple Choice:

1. a
2. b
3. d
4. b
5. a
6. c
7. b
8. b
9. d
10. a
11. c
12. d
13. c
14. a
15. c
16. d
17. c
18. c
19. c
20. d
21. a
22. c
23. d
24. d
25. c
26. b
27. b
28. a
29. a
30. d

True/False:

1. True
2. True
3. False
4. True
5. False
6. True
7. True
8. False
9. True
10. False
11. False
12. True
13. False
14. True
15. True
16. True
17. False
18. False
19. True
20. False
21. False
22. True
23. True
24. True
25. False

Matching:

1. f
2. k
3. p
4. o
5. b
6. t
7. m
8. h
9. d
10. e
11. q
12. a
13. j
14. n
15. g
16. r
17. i
18. c
19 l
20. s

False Statements Made True

3. In determining the rate to be paid for performing a job, the relative worth of the job is one of the **most** important factors to be considered.

5. The job descriptions and job specifications developed through job analysis should be as **accurate** as possible if they are to be of value to those who make human resources management (HRM) decisions.
8. The objective of the critical incident method of job analysis is to **identify critical job tasks**.
10. Skills that are **relevant** to a job include education or **experience**, specialized training, personal traits or abilities, and **manual** dexterities.
11. When writing a job description, it is essential to use statements that are **terse, direct, and simply worded**.
13. Job **enrichment**, or the vertical expansion of jobs, may be accomplished by increasing the autonomy and responsibility of employees.
17. Ergonomics **attempts to accommodate the human capabilities and limitations of those who are to perform a job. It is concerned with adapting the entire job system—the work, the work environment, the machine and equipment, and the processes—to match human characteristics**.
18. Ergonomics has recently focused on the **elimination, or at least the reduction**, of many repetitive motion injuries, particularly those related to the back and wrist.
20. Permanent groups of five to ten employees doing similar or related work who meet together regularly to identify, analyze, and suggest solutions to shared problems are often referred to as **employee involvement groups**.
21. **Synergy** occurs when the interactions and outcomes of team members are greater than the sum of their individual efforts.
25. A variant of telecommuting is the **virtual office** where employees are in the **field** selling to, or servicing, customers or are stationed at other remote locations working as if they were in the **home office**.

CHAPTER

5

EXPANDING THE TALENT POOL: RECRUITMENT AND CAREERS

In this chapter you will learn about multiple approaches to the recruiting process. Employers use internal promotion and transfer to fill as many positions as possible above the entry level. You will learn the relevance of career planning throughout your tenure of employment. It is important to understand that top management must support career development. You will understand the knowledge and skills needed to perform individual jobs. You will learn how assessment centers are used in the recruiting process. Finally, you will learn the advantages of belonging to a women's network.

LEARNING OBJECTIVES

After studying this chapter, you should be able to

1 Explain the advantages and disadvantages of external recruitment.

2 Explain the advantages and disadvantages of recruiting from within the organization.

3 Discuss how job opportunities can be inventoried and employee potential assessed.

4 Explain how career management programs intigrate the needs of individual employees and their organizations.

5 Describe the conditions that make career management programs successful.

6 Explain why diverse recruitment and career development activities are important to companies.

CHAPTER SUMMARY RELATING TO LEARNING OBJECTIVES

1 In order to expand the talent pool of organizations—the number and kinds of people available for employment—organizations must focus on multiple approaches to recruitment and career management. Outside sources for recruitment are especially useful for filling jobs with special qualifications and to acquire individuals with new skills, ideas, and perspectives. Which outside sources and methods are used in recruiting will depend on the recruitment goals of the organization, the conditions of the labor market, and the specifications of the jobs to be filled.

2 Employers usually find it advantageous to use internal promotion and transfer to fill as many openings as possible above the entry level. By recruiting from within, an organization they have made in recruiting, selecting, training, and developing its current employees. Further, internal promotions can reward employees for past performance and send a signal to other employees that their future efforts will pay off. However, potential candidates from the outside should occasionally be considered in order to prevent the inbreeding of ideas and attitudes.

The legal requirements governing EEO make it mandatory that employers proactively recruit and promote members of protected classes so that their representation at all levels within the organization will approximate their proportionate numbers in the labor market. These efforts include recruiting not only those members who are qualified but also those who can be made qualified with reasonable training and assistance.

3 Job opportunities may be identified by studying jobs and determining the knowledge and skills each one requires. Once that is accomplished, key jobs can be identified, and job progressions planned. These progressions can then serve as a basis for developing the career paths of employees. Once career paths are developed and employees are identified on the career ladders, it is possible to inventory the jobs and determine where individuals with the required skills and knowledge are or will be needed.

Identifying and developing managerial talent is a responsibility of all managers. In addition to immediate superiors, there should be others in the organization who can nominate and sponsor employees with promise. Many organizations use assessment centers to identify managerial talent and recommend developmental experiences so each individual can reach her or his full potential. Mentoring has been found to be valuable for providing guidance and support to potential managers.

4 Beyond recruiting per se, organizations also need to consider the progression of employees through a series of jobs. In this way, firms can manage not only the immediate contribution of an individual to the organization but the long-term contribution throughout their career. A career development program is a dynamic process that should integrate individual employee needs with those of the organization.

It is the responsibility of the employee to identify his or her own knowledge, skills, and aptitudes (KSAs) as well as interests and values and to seek out information about career options. The organization should provide information about its mission, policies, and plans and what it will provide in the way of training and development for the employee.

5 In order to be successful, a career management program must receive the support of a firm's top managers. The program should reflect the goals and culture of the organization, and managerial personnel at all levels must be trained in the fundamentals of job design, performance appraisal, career planning, and counseling. Employees should be aware of the organization's philosophy and its goals; otherwise they will not know how their goals match those of the organization. HRM policies, especially those related to rotation, transfers, and promotions of employees should be consistent with the firm's goals. The objectives and opportunities of the career development program should be announced widely throughout the organization.

The first step in facilitating the career development of women is to eliminate barriers to their advancement. Creating women's networks, providing special training for women, accepting women as valued members of the organization, providing mentors for women, and accommodating families have been found to be effective ways to facilitate a woman's career development.

6 A diversified workforce is composed of many different groups, an important segment of which is minority groups. In addition to creating conditions that are favorable for recognizing and rewarding the performance of employees, many organizations have special programs such as internships that provide hands-on experience as well as special training opportunities. Other groups that require the attention of management are the disabled, older workers, and dual-career couples, who often need to have flexible working option.

REVIEW QUESTIONS

Multiple Choice

1 ________ 1. The process of locating potential individuals who might join an organization, and encouraging them to apply for existing or anticipated job openings is

a. selection.
b. job evaluation.
c. recruitment.
d. job analysis.

1

_______ 2. Whether a particular job vacancy will be filled by someone from within the organization or from outside will depend upon
a. the availability of personnel.
b. the organization's HR policies.
c. the requirements of the job to be staffed.
d. all of the above.

1

_______ 3. One of the most common methods of attracting applicants is through
a. advertisements.
b. referrals.
c. friendship.
d. billboards.

1

_______ 4. The most commonly used search tactic by job seekers is the
a. radio.
b. Internet.
c. billboard.
d. transportation service.

1

_______ 5. Most job positions are filled through
a. word-of-mouth recommendations.
b. television ads.
c. billboard ads.
d. radio ads.

1

_______ 6. The practice of hiring relatives is referred to as
a. brotherhood.
b. fraternal care.
c. nepotism.
d. sisterhood.

1

_______ 7. A good source of young applicants with formal training but with relatively little full-time experience is
a. television.
b. radio.
c. billboard advertisements.
d. educational institutions.

1 _______ 8. A principle source of applicants for blue-collar and some professional jobs is
a. labor unions.
b. educational institutions.
c. television ads.
d. billboard advertisements.

1 _______ 9. Companies that place their employees with subscribers on a permanent basis are
a. employee-leasing firms.
b. educational services.
c. labor unions.
d. billboards.

1 _______ 10. The percentage of applicants from a particular source that make it to the next stage in the selection process is called a
a. labor utility.
b. yield ratio.
c. recruiter.
d. labor-to-hour ratio.

1 _______ 11. Applicants are informed about all aspects of the job, including both its desirable and undesirable facets, with a
a. selection device.
b. labor turnover.
c. test.
d. realistic job preview (RJP).

1 _______ 12. According to the Society for Human Resource Management , companies with fewer than 50 employees can save from $5000 to $50,000 in time an labor costs annually
a. by hiring a PEO.
b. by reducing labor turnover.
c. by offshoring.
d. through realistic job previews (RJP).

3 _______ 13. Many companies have developed online job posting systems whereby employees looking for upgraded positions can post their names, resumes, and the positions they are interested in applying for through a process referred to as
a. bumping.
b. job posting and bidding.

c. promotion.
d. job bidding.

3 _______ 14. A process by which individuals are evaluated as they participate in a series of situations that resemble what they might be called upon to handle on the job is called an
a. assessment center.
b. employee turnover.
c. advertisement.
d. application.

3 _______ 15. An activity where trainees are gathered in a conference room setting to discuss an assigned topic, either with or without designated group roles is called
a. role play
b. leaderless group discussion
c. behavioral interview
d. stress interview

4 _______ 16. What is a dynamic process that matches the needs of the organization which the needs of the employee?
a. leaderless group discussion
b. behavioral interview
c. career development program
d. assessment center

4 _______ 17. Career development programs benefit managers by giving them
a. increased skill in managing their own careers.
b. greater retention of valued employees.
c. increased understanding of the organization.
d. all of the above.

5 _______ 18. Lines of advancement for individuals in an occupational field within an organization are
a. employee cards.
b. career paths.
c. application turnovers.
d. career plans.

5 ______ 19. A change of assignment to a job at a higher level in the organization is a
a. bumping right.
b. promotion.
c. demotion.
d. transfer.

5 ______ 20. The placement of an employee in another job for which the duties, responsibilities, status, and remuneration are approximately equal to those of the previous job is a
a. transfer.
b. promotion.
c. demotion.
d. bumping procedure.

5 ______ 21. The placement of an employee into a lower-level job that can provide developmental opportunities is a
a. transfer.
b. promotion.
c. demotion.
d. bumping procedure.

5 ______ 22. Relocation services include all of the following *except*
a. moving expenses.
b. spouse transfer.
c. cultural orientation.
d. language training.

5 ______ 23. Organizations provide job-finding help for terminated employees through
a. recruitment.
b. selection.
c. retraining.
d. outplacement services.

5 ______ 24. A situation in which, either for organizational or personal reasons, the probability of moving up the career ladder is low is called a
a. career plan.
b. promotion.
c. career plateau.
d. demotion.

5

_______ 25. A plateau that marks the end of possible promotions, meaning an employee will have to leave the organization to find new opportunities and challenges, is termed
a. career planning.
b. structural plateauing.
c. career developing.
d. career paths.

5

_______ 26. Executives and managers who coach, advise, and encourage employees of lesser rank are called
a. managers.
b. executives.
c. mentors.
d. trainees.

6

_______ 27. The largest protected class is
a. women.
b. men.
c. trainees.
d. senior managers.

6

_______ 28. The most frequently cited advantage of employing people with disabilities is
a. their superior attendance.
b. their loyalty.
c. the low turnover rate.
d. all of the above.

6

_______ 29. The most frequent organizational accommodation to dual-career couples is
a. flextime.
b. street time.
c. promotion.
d. flexible working schedules.

6

_______ 30. The main problem faced by dual-career couples is
a. flextime.
b. threat of relocation
c. promotion.
d. flexible working schedules.

TRUE/FALSE

Identify the following statements as True or False.

1 _______ 1. During periods of low unemployment, organizations may be able to maintain an adequate supply of qualified applicants from unsolicited resumes alone.

1 _______ 2. In general, applicants who find employment through referral by a current employee tend to remain with the organization longer.

1 _______ 3. Formal recruiting sources may yield higher selection rates than informal sources.

1 _______ 4. The preparation of recruiting advertisements is time consuming and requires creativity in developing design and message content.

1 _______ 5. If there is no possibility of employment in the organization at present or in the future, the applicant should be tactfully and frankly informed of this fact.

1 _______ 6. Managers have found that the quality of employee-referred applicants is normally quite low since employees are generally hesitant to recommend individuals.

1 _______ 7. One of the best ways to publicize a referral program is to celebrate successes.

1 _______ 8. New data suggest that CEOs who are promoted from within their organizations actually outperform those hired from the outside.

1 _______ 9. About 80 percent of the workers in the United States hold bachelor's degrees—about the same percentage as in 1980.

1 _______ 10. Individuals who become unemployed must register at a local public employment office and be available for "suitable employment" in order to receive their weekly unemployment checks.

1 _______ 11. Increasingly, temps are being employed to fill positions once staffed by permanent employees because temporaries can be laid off quickly, and with less cost, when work lessens.

3 _______ 12. In role playing, the interviewer asks the participant a series of questions about what he or she would do in particular work circumstances.

4 ________ 13. Because having a successful career involves creating your own career path, it is up to each individual to identify his or her own knowledge, skills, abilities, interests, and values and seek out information about career options in order to set goals and develop career plans.

4 ________ 14. One of the most important indicators of management support comes in the form of mentoring.

5 ________ 15. The three principal criteria for determining promotions are merit, seniority, and personality.

5 ________ 16. A downward transfer, or *demotion*, moves an individual into a lateral job that can provide developmental opportunities.

5 ________ 17. Demotions require individuals to adjust to new job demands and usually to a different work environment.

5 ________ 18. Individuals pursuing boundaryless careers develop their knowledge in ways specific to a given firm.

6 ________ 19. Career counseling involves talking with employees about their current job activities and performance, their personal and career interests and goals, their personal skills, and suitable career development objectives.

6 ________ 20. A fast-track program may provide for a relatively rapid progression—lateral transfers or promotions—through a number of managerial positions requiring exposure to different organizational functions.

6 ________ 21. Career self-management training is geared to skills and behaviors associated with a specific job.

6 ________ 22. Most mentoring relationships develop quickly on a formal basis.

6 ________ 23. As a complement to mentoring, where relationships are more selective, networking relationships tend to be more varied and temporary.

7 ________ 24. Research has shown that fewer male managers tend to be more receptive to the advancement of women managers.

7 ________ 25. The U.S. Department of Labor defines the glass ceiling as "those artificial barriers based on attitudinal or organizational bias that prevent qualified individuals from advancing upward in their organizations into management-level positions."

Matching

Match each term with the proper definition.

Terms

a.	assessment center	k.	nepotism
b.	career counseling	l.	outplacement services
c.	career paths	m.	promotion
d.	career plateau	n.	relocation services
e.	dual-career partnerships	o.	realistic job preview (RJP)
f.	employee leasing	p.	transfer
g.	fast-track program	q.	yield ratio
h.	job posting and bidding	r.	career networking
i.	job progressions	s.	entrepreneur
j.	mentors		

Definitions

_______ 1. posting vacancy notices and maintaining lists of employees looking for upgraded positions

_______ 2. a preference for hiring relatives of current employees

_______ 3. process of dismissing employees who are then hired by a leasing company (which handles all HR-related activities) and contracting with that company to lease back the employees

_______ 4. percentage of applicants from a recruitment source that make it to the next stage of the selection process

_______ 5. informing applicants about all aspects of the job, including both its desirable and undesirable facets

_______ 6. hierarchy of jobs a new employee might experience, ranging from a starting job to jobs that successively require more knowledge and/or skill

_______ 7. lines of advancement in an occupational field within an organization

_______ 8. change of assignment to a job at a higher level in the organization

_______ 9. placement of an individual in another job for which the duties, responsibilities, status, and remuneration are approximately equal to those of the previous job

_______ 10. services provided to an employee who is transferred to a new location, which might include help in moving, in selling a home, in orienting to a new culture, and/or in learning a new language

_______ 11. services provided by organizations to help terminated employees find a new job

_______ 12. process by which individuals are evaluated as they participate in a series of situations that resemble what they might be called upon to handle on the job

_______ 13. process of discussing with employees their current job activities and performance, their personal and career interests and goals, their personal skills, and suitable career development objectives

_______ 14. program that encourages young managers with high potential to remain with an organization by enabling them to advance more rapidly than those with less potential

_______ 15. executives who coach, advise, and encourage individuals of lesser rank

_______ 16. couples in which both members follow their own careers and actively support each other's career development

_______ 17. situation in which for either organizational or personal reasons the probability of moving up the career ladder is low

_______ 18. process of establishing mutually beneficial relationships with other business people, including potential clients and customers.

_______ 19. One who starts, organizes, managers, and assumes responsibility for a business or other enterprise

Internet Exercises

What are some of the current policy provisions of relocation services for employees?
http://www.fpd.finop.umn.edu/groups/ppd/documents/policy/Moving.cfm.

Is there hope for dual-career couples to find satisfaction in all aspects of their lives?
http://physics.wm.edu/dualcareer.html.

How to Form an Effective Mentoring Relationship

In forming an effective mentoring relationship, you should:

1. Research the person's background.
2. Have someone introduce you or get involved with your mentor in a business setting.
3. Let your mentor know you admire him or her.
4. Keep in mind that mentoring is a two-way exchange.
5. Arrange a meeting and set goals, listen attentively, and ask questions.
6. Follow up, try the suggestions, and share the results.
7. Request an ongoing relationship by meeting on a regular basis.

SOLUTIONS

Multiple Choice:	True/False	Matching:
1. c	1. False	1. h
2. a	2. True	2. k
3. a	3. False	3. f
4. b	4. True	4. q
5. a	5. True	5. o
6. c	6. False	6. i
7. d	7. True	7. c
8. a	8. True	8. m
9. a	9. False	9. p
10. b	10. True	10. n
11. d	11. True	11. l
12. a	12. False	12. a
13. b	13. True	13. b
14. a	14. True	14. g
15. b	15. False	15. j
16. c	16. False	16. e
17. d	17. True	17. d
18. b	18. False	18. r
19. b	19. True	19. s
20. a	20. True	
21. c	21. False	
22. b	22. False	
23. d	23. True	
24. c	24. False	
25. b	25. True	
26. c		
27. a		
28. d		
29. d		
30. b		

False Statements Made True

1. During periods of **high** unemployment, organizations may be able to maintain an adequate supply of qualified applicants from unsolicited resumes alone.
3. **Informal** recruiting sources may yield higher selection rates than **formal** sources.
6. Managers have found that the quality of employee-referred applicants is normally quite **high** since employees are generally hesitant to recommend individuals.
9. About **30** percent of the workers in the United States hold bachelor's degrees—about the same percentage as in 1980.
12. In **behavioral interviews**, the interviewer asks the participant a series of questions about what he or she would do in particular work circumstances
15. The three principal criteria for determining promotions are merit, seniority, and **potential**.
16. A downward transfer, or *demotion*, moves an individual into a **lower-level** job that can provide developmental opportunities.
18. Individuals pursuing **more traditional** careers develop their knowledge in ways specific to a given firm.
21. Career self-management training **is not** geared to skills and behaviors associated with a specific job.
22. Most mentoring relationships develop **over time** on an **informal** basis.
24. Research has shown that **newer** male managers tend to be more receptive to the advancement of women managers.

PART THREE

Developing Effectiveness in Human Resources

CHAPTER

6

EMPLOYEE SELECTION

This chapter emphasizes the importance of personnel selection in the building of a productive workforce. Determining the qualifications of job candidates requires that as much information as possible be obtained from the candidates and other sources. Such information should be relevant to the job and sufficiently reliable and valid. It is essential that interviewers are thoroughly trained in how to obtain the information needed and how to avoid being discriminatory. Human resources practitioners need to understand job requirements in order to evaluate application forms, employment tests, interviews, and reference checks of individual candidates.

LEARNING OBJECTIVES

After studying this chapter, you should be able to

1 Explain the objectives of the personnel selection process.

2 Identify the various sources of information used for personnel selection.

3 Compare the value of different types of employment tests.

4 Illustrate the different approaches to conducting an employment interview.

5 Describe the various decision strategies for selection.

CHAPTER SUMMARY RELATING TO LEARNING OBJECTIVES

1 The employee selection process should provide as much reliable and valid information as possible about applicants so that their qualifications can be carefully matched with job's specifications. The information that is obtained should be clearly job related or predict success on the job and free from potential discrimination. *Reliability* refers to the consistency of test scores over time and across measures. *Validity* refers to the accuracy of measurements taken. Validity can be assessed in terms of whether the measurement is based on a job specification (content validity), whether test scores correlate with performance criteria (predictive validity), and whether the test accurately measures what it purports to measure (construct validity).

2 Interviews are customarily used in conjunction with application forms, biographical information blanks, references, background investigations, medical examinations, cognitive ability tests, job knowledge tests, and work sample tests.

3 While the popularity of employment tests declined somewhat with the passage of Equal Employment Opportunity (EEO) laws, following 9-11, there was a resurgence of testing. Employment test should not be overlooked because they are more objective than the interview and can give managers a fuller, or better, sense of the capabilities of different candidates. Cognitive ability tests are especially valuable for assessing verbal, quantitative, and reasoning abilities. Personality and interest tests are perhaps best used for placement or career development. Physical ability tests can be used to prevent accidents and injuries, particularly for physically demanding work. However, they must not be used if they have a disparate impact on candidates in protected classes. Job knowledge and work sample tests are achievement tests that are useful for determining whether a candidate can perform the duties of the job without further training.

4 The interview is an important source of information about job applicants. It can be unstructured, wherein the interviewer is free to pursue whatever approach and sequence of topics might seem appropriate, as long as they are job related. Alternatively, an interview can be structured, wherein each applicant receives the same set of questions, which have pre-established answers associated with different scores. Some interviews are situational and questions can focus on hypothetical situations or actual behavioral descriptions of a candidate's previous work experiences. Interviews can be conducted by a single individual, by a panel, or via a computer or be videotaped or digitally recorded. Regardless of the technique chosen, those who conduct interviews should receive special training to acquaint them with interviewing methods and Equal Employment Opportunity (EEO) considerations. The training should also make them more aware of the major findings from research studies on the interview and how they can apply these findings and avoid biases.

5 In the process of making decisions, all "can-do" and "will-do" factors should be assembled and weighted systematically so that the final decision can be based on a composite of the most reliable and valid information. Although the clinical approach to decision making is used more than the statistical approach, the former lacks the accuracy of the latter. Compensatory models allow a candidate's high score on one predictor to make up for a low score on another. When the multiple cutoffs model is used, only those candidates who score above a minimum cutoff level remain in the running. A variation of the multiple cutoff is the multiple hurdle model, which involves several stages and cutoff levels. Whichever of these approaches is used, the goal is to select a greater proportion of individuals who will be successful on the job.

REVIEW QUESTIONS

Multiple Choice

Choose the letter of the word or phrase that best completes each statement.

1 _______ 1. The process of choosing individuals who have relevant qualifications to fill existing jobs or projected job openings is known as
   a. job fit.
   b. job analysis.
   c. selection.
   d. recruiting.

1 _______ 2. The selection procedure is generally the responsibility of the Human Resources (HR) Department; however, the final decision about hiring a person in their department is made by
   a. operating employees.
   b. line managers.
   c. staff managers.
   d. management consultants.

1 _______ 3. The extent to which two or more selection methods (interviews and tests, for example) yield similar results or are consistent is referred to as
a. reliability.
b. content validity.
c. predictive validity.
d. concurrent validity.

1 _______ 4. Performance on a test, when compared with actual production records and other measures that are appropriate to each type of job, is an example of
a. cross-functional validity.
b. internal reliability.
c. compensatory models.
d. criterion-related validity.

1 _______ 5. The two types of criterion-related validity are
a. concurrent and predictive.
b. content and internal reliability.
c. predictive and cross-validity.
d. face and construct validity.

1 _______ 6. Where it is not feasible to use the criterion-related approach, often because of limited samples of individuals, the method used is
a. faith validity.
b. reliability.
c. construct validity.
d. content validity.

2 _______ 7. One of the oldest methods for predicting job success of job applicants is
a. educational data.
b. hobbies and interests.
c. employment history.
d. biographical information.

2 _______ 8. What can companies be held liable for if they fail to make adequate background checks?
a. negligent hiring
b. discrimination
c. violation of affirmative action laws
d. undue hardship.

2 _______ 9. A device that measures the changes in breathing, blood pressure, and pulse of a person who is being questioned is a(n)
a. polygraph machine.
b. assessment center.
c. achievement test.
d. personality test.

2 _______ 10. In response to the Employee Polygraph Protection Act, many employers have dramatically increased their use of
a. educational data.
b. honesty and integrity tests
c. graphology.
d. biographical information.

2 _______ 11. One of the later steps in the selection process, because of its cost, is the
a. interview.
b. background investigation.
c. employment test.
d. medical examination.

2 _______ 12. The normal method of drug testing used by employers is
a. a biographical test.
b. a personality test.
c. urine sampling.
d. a hair follicle test.

3 _______ 13. An objective and standardized measure of a sample of behavior that is used to gauge a person's knowledge, skills, abilities, and other characteristics is a(n)
a. application form.
b. physical exam.
c. background investigation.
d. employment test.

3 _______ 14. The type of employment test that measures a person's capacity to learn or acquire skills is a(n)
a. aptitude test.
b. work sample.
c. assessment center.
d. achievement test.

3 _______ 15. The instrument that measures mental capabilities such as general intelligence, verbal fluency, numerical ability, and reasoning ability is a(n)
a. personality test.
b. achievement test.
c. cognitive ability test.
d. assessment center.

3 _______ 16. The Scholastic Aptitude Test (SAT) and the Graduate Management Admission Test (GMAT) are examples of a(n)
a. personality test.
b. achievement test.
c. cognitive ability test.
d. assessment center.

3 _______ 17. The type of instrument that measures disposition characteristics such as extroversion, agreeableness, conscientiousness, emotional stability, and openness to experience is a(n)
a. achievement test.
b. personality test.
c. aptitude test.
d. work sample test.

3 _______ 18. The Meyers-Briggs Type Indicator (MBTI) is a well known
a. personality test.
b. achievement test.
c. cognitive ability test.
d. assessment center.

4 _______ 19. The mainstay of employment selection is the interview because of he following, *except*
a. the small number of applicants.
b. interviewer judgment.
c. internal bias.
d. good public relations.

4 _______ 20. The type of interview in which the interviewer carefully refrains from influencing the applicant's remarks and the applicant is allowed the maximum amount of freedom in determining the course of the discussion is the
a. nondirective interview.
b. structured interview.
c. situational interview.
d. stress interview.

4 _______ 21. The type of interview that has a set of standardized questions (based on job analysis) and an established set of answers against which applicant responses can be rated and provides a more consistent basis for evaluating job candidates is the
a. situational interview.
b. nondirective interview.
c. structured interview.
d. assessment center.

4 _______ 22. The interviewing technique in which the applicant is given a hypothetical incident and asked how he or she would respond is known as a
a. nondirective interview.
b. situational interview.
c. structured guide interview.
d. work sample interview.

4 _______ 23. A selection technique in which a board of recruiters is attempting to poll a candidate is called a
a. situational interview.
b. behavioral interview.
c. structured guide interview.
d. panel interview.

5 _______ 24. While all of the steps in the selection process are important, the most critical step is the decision to
a. accept or reject applicants.
b. utilize employment tests.
c. use application forms.
d. administer reference checks.

5 _______ 25. An evaluation of candidates on the basis of assembled information should focus on the factors of
a. skills and aptitude analysis.
b. can-do and will-do candidate analysis.
c. achievement and potential analysis.
d. job analysis and position descriptions.

5 _______ 26. The approach in which those making the selection decision review all the data on applicants before making the candidate choice is the
a. statistical approach.
b. biographical approach.
c. clinical approach.
d. work sample analysis.

5 _______ 27. The selection decision that requires an applicant to achieve some level of proficiency on all selection dimensions is called the
a. job analysis.
b. job specification.
c. multiple cutoff model.
d. job description.

5 _______ 28. The number of applicants compared with the number of persons to be hired is called the
a. selection ratio.
b. panel interview.
c. situational interview.
d. job description.

5 _______ 29. After a preliminary selection has been made in the employment department, those applicants who appear to be most promising are then referred to departments having vacancies; there they are interviewed by the department managers, who usually make the
a. contract offer.
b. final hiring decision.
c. performance evaluation.
d. training criteria.

5 _______ 30. Choosing someone because you are in a pinch is called
a. contract offer.
b. desperation bias.
c. performance bias.
d. ratee bias.

True/False

Identify the following statements as True or False.

1 _______ 1. In a person-organization fit, managers will pass up potential employees if they don't embrace the values of the organization.

1 _______ 2. In most organizations, selection is an ongoing process for the human resources specialist.

1 _______ 3. A selection procedure never should be validated before it is used.

1 _______ 4. Research has proven that validity coefficients can often be generalized across situations.

1 _______ 5. The closer the content of the selection instrument is to actual work samples or behaviors, the greater its content validity.

1 _______ 6. The extent to which a selection tool measures a theoretical construct, or trait, is known as construct validity.

2 _______ 7. Most organizations require application forms to be completed because they provide a fairly quick and systematic means of obtaining a variety of information about the applicant.

2 _______ 8. The only purpose of an application form is to provide information for deciding whether an applicant meets the minimum requirements of the job being offered.

2 _______ 9. Both the biographical information blanks (BIB) and the application form can be scored like tests, and because biographical questions rarely have obviously right or wrong answers, BIBs are difficult to fake.

2 _______ 10. Reference checking is commonly used to screen and select applicants and has always been successful in predicting employee performance.

2 _______ 11. Graphology refers to a variety of systems of handwriting analysis; however, it is never used by employers to make employment decisions.

3 _______ 12. The number of U.S. companies that test employment candidates for drug use has decreased significantly.

3 _______ 13. While high reliability is essential, it offers no assurance that the test provides the basis for making valid judgments.

3 _______ 14. Achievement tests require the applicant to perform tasks that are actually a part of the work required on the job.

3 _______ 15. Despite their potential value, physical ability tests tend to work to the disadvantage of women and job applicants with disabilities.

4 _______ 16. In using the nondirective interview approach, the interviewer listens carefully and does not argue with or interrupt the candidate or change the subject abruptly.

4 _______ 17. A structured interview is more likely to provide the type of information needed for making sound decisions; however, it increases the likelihood of legal charges of unfair discrimination.

4 _______ 18. A behavioral description interview focuses on actual work incidents in the interviewee's past and on what the job applicant has done in a given job situation.

4 _______ 19. The panel interview consists of three to five recruiters interviewing a group of potential employees at the same time.

5 _______ 20. Video interviews have several potential advantages related to flexibility, speed, and cost.

5 _______ 21. The decision strategy for selecting managerial and executive personnel will differ from the strategy used in selecting clerical and technical personnel.

5 _______ 22. In the statistical approach to decision making, those making the selection decision review all the data on applicants.

5 _______ 23. The clinical approach to decision making involves identifying the most valid predictors and weighting them through clinical methods such as multiple regression analysis.

5 _______ 24. The statistical approach to employment decisions includes compensatory, multiple cutoff, and multiple hurdle models.

5 _______ 25. In large organizations, notifying applicants of the decision and making job offers is often the responsibility of the HR department.

Matching

Match each term with the proper definition.

Terms

a. achievement tests
b. aptitude tests
c. behavioral description interview (BDI)
d. compensatory model
e. concurrent validity
f. construct validity
g. content validity
h. criterion-related validity
i. cross-validation
j. multiple cutoff model
k. multiple hurdle model
l. nondirective interview
m. panel interview
n. predictive validity
o. reliability
p. selection
q. selection ratio
r. situational interview
s. structured interview
t. validity
u. validity generalization
v. negligent hiring

Definitions

_______ 1. the process of choosing individuals who have relevant qualifications to fill existing or projected job openings

_______ 2. an interview in which an applicant is asked about what he or she actually did in a given situation

_______ 3. the extent to which applicants' test scores match criterion data obtained from those applicants/employees after they have been on the job for some indefinite period

_______ 4. an interview in which the applicant is allowed the maximum amount of freedom in determining the course of the discussion, while the interviewer carefully refrains from influencing the applicant's remarks

_______ 5. measures of what a person knows or can do right now

_______ 6. the extent to which test scores (or other predictor information) match criterion data obtained at about the same time from current employees

_______ 7. a sequential strategy in which only applicants with the highest scores at an initial test stage go on to subsequent stages

_______ 8. the degree to which interviews, tests, and other selection procedures yield comparable data over time and alternative measures

_______ 9. measures of a person's capacity to learn or acquire skills

_______ 10. the extent to which validity coefficients can be generalized across situations

_______ 11. the extent to which a selection instrument, such as a test, adequately samples the knowledge and skills needed to perform a particular job

_______ 12. an interview in which an applicant is given a hypothetical incident and asked how he or she would respond to it

_______ 13. degree to which a test or selection procedure measures a person's attributes

_______ 14. verifying the results obtained from a validation study by administering a test or test battery to a different sample (drawn from the same population)

_______ 15. an interview in which a board of interviewers questions and observes a single candidate

_______ 16. selection decision model in which a high score in one area can make up for a low score in another area

_______ 17. the number of applicants compared with the number of persons hired

_______ 18. the extent to which a selection tool predicts, or significantly correlates with, important elements of work behavior

_______ 19. selection decision model that requires an applicant to achieve some minimum level of proficiency on all selection dimensions

_______ 20. an interview in which a set of standardized questions with an established set of answers is used

_______ 21. the extent to which a selection tool measures a theoretical construct or trait

_______ 22. What companies can be held liable for if they fail to make adequate background checks

Internet Exercises

Why are employment tests so critical?
http://www.findarticles.com/p/articles/mi_m3495/is_2_47/ai_83058935/print.
Why are situational interviews so helpful to employers?
http://www.findarticles.com/p/articles/mi_m0DTI/is_1_32/ai_n9778435/print.

How to Effectively Write a Resume and Successfully Prepare for an Interview

1. You should understand the guidelines for an effective resume. A resume should include:

- *Personal identification information:* List your name, address, telephone number, email address, and so on.
- *Resume objectives:* What are you looking for in terms of a job? Relate these objectives to your career goals.
- *Education:* This section should support and be directly correlated with your objectives. Include courses taken as well as specific skills developed through these courses, such as computer skills, problem-solving skills, and communication skills.
- *Work experience:* This information should relate to the occupational fields in which you have worked. Make sure this information indicates that you have held a job over a period of time. Highlight transferable skills related to leadership, conflict resolution, time management, and stress management activities.
- *Awards, activities, and/or military experience:* Include community experience, voluntarism (food banks, scouting programs, etc.), and/or professional memberships, such as Rotary, Kiwanis, Lions, etc.

2. To develop a competitive advantage in preparation for an interview, you should do the following:

- *Research the firm:* The library and Chamber of Commerce are excellent sources of information pertaining to a local business enterprise. Two specific sources are *The Wall Street Journal*'s "Index to Businesses" and *Standard and Poor's* "Industry Surveys."
- *Complete application forms:* Use proper English grammar and spelling. Answer all application questions at the appropriate level of detail.
- *Prepare for the interview:* Anticipate questions pertaining to your level of education, work experience, and awards and activities. Have questions for the recruiter following the interview, such as: How soon do you plan to fill this position? What growth opportunities, career development programs, orientation and training activities, and so on are available?
- *References and background investigations:* Ask for permission before using any individual's name for a reference.

SOLUTIONS

Multiple Choice:	True/False:	Matching:
1. c	1. True	1. p
2. b	2. True	2. c
3. a	3. False	3. n
4. d	4. True	4. l
5. a	5. True	5. a
6. d	6. True	6. e
7. d	7. True	7. k
8. a	8. False	8. o
9. a	9. True	9. b
10. b	10. False	10. u
11. d	11. False	11. g
12. c	12. False	12. r
13. d	13. True	13. t
14. a	14. False	14. i
15. c	15. True	15. m
16. c	16. True	16. d
17. b	17. False	17. q
18. a	18. True	18. h
19. c	19. False	19. j
20. a	20. True	20. s
21. c	21. True	21. f
22. b	22. False	22. v
23. d	23. False	
24. a	24. True	
25. b	25. True	
26. c		
27. c		
28. a		
29. b		
30. b		

False Statements Made True

3. A selection procedure **must** be validated before it is used.
8. **One of the several purposes** of an application form is to provide information for deciding whether an applicant meets the minimum requirements of the job being offered.
10. Reference checking is commonly used to screen and select applicants **but has not proven successful** in predicting employee performance.
11. Graphology refers to a variety of systems of handwriting analysis **and is used by some** employers to make employment decisions.
12. The number of U.S. companies that test employment candidates for drug use has **increased** significantly.
14. Achievement tests **measure what a person knows or can do right now**.
17. A structured interview is more likely to provide the type of information needed for making sound decisions**; it also reduces the possibility** of legal charges of unfair discrimination.
19. The panel interview consists of three to five recruiters interviewing a **single candidate**.
22. In the **clinical** approach to decision making, those making the selection decision review all the data on applicants.
23. The **statistical** approach to decision making involves identifying the most valid predictors and weighting them through **statistical** methods such as multiple regression analysis.

CHAPTER 7

TRAINING AND DEVELOPMENT

In this chapter, you will learn the systems approach to training and development and be able to describe the components of training-needs assessment. You will be able to identify the principles of learning and explain how they facilitate training. In this chapter, you will learn the types of training methods used for managers and nonmanagers. You will be able to discuss the advantages and disadvantages of various evaluation criteria. Finally, you will learn about the special training programs that are currently popular.

LEARNING OBJECTIVES

After studying this chapter, you should be able to

1. Discuss the systems approach to training and development.
2. Describe the components of training-needs assessment.
3. Identify the principles of learning and describe how they facilitate training.
4. Identify the types of training methods used for managers and nonmanagers.
5. Discuss the advantages and disadvantages of various evaluation criteria.
6. Describe the special training programs that are currently popular.

CHAPTER SUMMARY RELATING TO LEARNING OBJECTIVES

1 Today we find that organizational operations cover a broad range of subjects and involve personnel at all levels, from orientation through management development. In order to have effective job training programs, the systems approach is recommended. This approach has four phases: (1) needs assessment, (2) program design, (3) implementation, and (4) evaluation.

2 Needs assessment begins with organization analysis. Managers must establish a context for training by deciding where training is needed, how it connects with strategic goals, and how their companies' resources can best be used in terms of training. A task analysis is used to identify the knowledge, skills, and abilities need. A person analysis is used to identify which people need training.

3 When designing a training program, managers must consider the two fundamental preconditions for learning: the readiness and motivation of trainees. In addition, the principles of learning should be considered in order to create an environment that is conducive to learning. These principles include goal setting, the meaningfulness of presentation, modeling, individual differences, active practice and repetition, whole-versus-part learning, massed versus distributed learning, and feedback and reinforcement.

4 A wide variety of methods are available to train nonmanagerial personnel. On-the-job training is one of the most commonly used methods because it provides trainees with hands-on experience and an opportunity to build a relationship with their supervisor and coworkers. Apprenticeship training and internships are especially effective because they provide both on- and off-the-job experiences. Other off-the-job methods include classroom training, programmed instruction, computer-based training, simulations and, interactive e-learning utilizing teleconferencing, video conferencing, webinars, and the communities of practice method of learning. Using multiple methods, or what is called blended learning, has been found to be most effective.

The training and development of managers is becoming increasingly critical for firms because they are facing increase competition from across the globe and the baby boomers generation in the United States is retiring. As with nonmanagerial personnel, a wide variety of training methods are used for developing managers. On-the-job experiences include coaching, understudy assignment, job rotation, lateral transfer, project and committee assignments, and staff meetings. Off-the-job experiences include analysis of case studies, management games and simulations, role-playing, and behavior modeling.

5 Evaluation of a training program should focus on several criteria: participant reactions, learning, behavior change on the job, and bottom-line results such as return on investment. Transfer of training is measured via examination of the degree to which trained skills are demonstrated back on the job. Benchmarking and utility analysis help evaluate the impact of training and provide the information for further needs assessment.

6 Special issues in training involve those programs that are important to a broad range of employees. Orientation training, for example, begins and continues throughout an employee's service with an organization. By participating in a formal orientation program, employees acquire the knowledge, skills, and attitudes that increase the probability of their success with the organization. To make an orientation effective, there should be close cooperation between the Human Resources Department and other departments in all phases of the program, from initial planning through follow-up and evaluation. Basic skills training, team training, ethics training, and diversity training are also critically important in today's organizations.

REVIEW QUESTIONS

Multiple Choice

Choose the letter of the word or phrase that best completes each statement.

1 _______ 1. The process most often used to describe almost any effort initiated by an organization to foster learning among its members is

a. orientation.
b. training.
c. performance appraisal.
d. job evaluation.

1 _______ 2. Before initiating a training program, to ensure their firms' training dollars are spent wisely, about half of managers surveyed by the Institute of Management and Administration (IOMA) say their companies engage in

a. needs assessment.
b. setting goals and objectives.
c. evaluating training programs.
d. training feedback.

2 ______ 3. The top company executive responsible for making certain that training is timely and focused on the firm's top strategic issues is the
a. chief learning officer.
b. chief executive officer
c. chief ethics officer
d. chief training officer

2 ______ 4. The examination of the environment, strategies, and resources of the organization to determine where training emphasis should be placed is
a. management by objectives.
b. critical incident.
c. organization analysis.
d. job ranking.

2 ______ 5. Reviewing the job description and specifications to identify the activities needed to perform a particular job and the knowledge, skills, and aptitudes needed to perform those activities involves
a. personality enhancement.
b. the socialization process.
c. behavior modification.
d. task analysis.

2 ______ 6. This focuses on the set of skills and knowledge employees need to be successful, particularly for decision-oriented and knowledge-intensive jobs.
a. personality assessment.
b. the socialization assessment.
c. behavior assessment.
d. competency assessment.

2 ______ 7. The process of determining which individual employees need training and which individuals do not is
a. person analysis.
b. job evaluation.
c. job analysis.
d. employee orientation.

2 ________ 8. The success of a firm's training program is dependent upon
a. employee orientation.
b. performance appraisal.
c. job analysis.
d. training design.

2 ________ 9. As a result of conducting organization task and person analyses, managers will have a more complete picture of the training needs when they can state the desired outcomes of training through written
a. employee contracts.
b. job specifications.
c. instructional objectives.
d. implied contracts.

2 ________ 10. Two preconditions for learning affecting the success of those who are to receive training are
a. readiness and motivation.
b. task identity and task significance.
c. behavior and personality.
d. culture and the socialization process.

3 ________ 11. Training programs are likely to be more effective if they incorporate the
a. principles of learning.
b. orientation program.
c. selection process.
d. assessment program.

4 ________ 12. As an employee's training progresses, feedback serves two related purposes, which are
a. employee probation and career development.
b. knowledge of results and employee motivation.
c. job security and job protection.
d. employee results and performance evaluation.

4 ________ 13. Training that provides both hands-on experience under normal working conditions and opportunities for the trainer, manager, or senior employee to build good relationships with new employees is called
a. cooperative training.
b. on-the-job training.

c. competency assessment.
d. behavior modification.

4 _______ 14. The most common training method used to train nonmanagerial employees is
a. simulation training.
b. on-the-job training.
c. e-learning.
d. behavior modification

4 _______ 15. Training programs that require cooperation between organizations and their labor unions, between industry and government, or between organizations and local school systems are
a. work seminars.
b. career development programs.
c. job rotation activities.
d. apprenticeship programs.

4 _______ 16. The type of training that combines practical on-the-job experience with formal classes is known as
a. on-the-job training.
b. vestibule training.
c. job instruction training.
d. cooperative training.

4 _______ 17. A program that is jointly sponsored by colleges, universities, and a variety of organizations and that offers students the chance to get real-world experience while finding out how they will perform in work settings is a(n)
a. coaching technique.
b. mentor.
c. performance evaluation.
d. internship program.

4 _______ 18. Training that is particularly effective in allowing individual trainees to work at their own pace is called
a. on-the-job training.
b. programmed instruction.
c. apprenticeship training.
d. cooperative training.

4 _______ 19. The audiovisual, programmed, and computer-oriented training methods are evolving into what trainers today refer to as
a. e-learning.
b. on-the-job training.
c. job instruction.
d. vestibule training.

4 _______ 20. A training method that emphasizes realism in equipment and its operation at minimum cost and maximum safety is known as a(n)
a. internship program.
b. on-the-job training program.
c. work sampling method.
d. simulation method.

4 _______ 21. Assuming the attitudes and behavior of others involved in a particular problem is known as
a. job instruction training.
b. role playing.
c. orientation.
d. anxiety training.

4 _______ 22. What term is used to describe training methods that use multiple techniques?
a. job instruction training.
b. role playing.
c. orientation.
d. blended learning

5 _______ 23. The following basic criteria are available to evaluate training programs, *except*
a. learning.
b. predictions.
c. behavior.
d. results.

5 _______ 24. One of the simplest and most common approaches to training evaluation is assessing
a. employee needs.
b. leadership styles.
c. coaching techniques.
d. participant reactions.

6 _______ 25. Managers must clearly define the measures of competency and performance and must objectively assess the current situation and identify areas for improvement when using
a. quality circles.
b. vestibule training.
c. benchmarking.
d. on-the-job training.

6 _______ 26. The formal process of familiarizing new employees with the organization, their jobs, and their work unit is
a. team training.
b. diversity training.
c. sensitivity training.
d. orientation training.

6 _______ 27. Learning essential occupational qualifications having profound implications for product quality, customer service, internal efficiency, and workplace and environmental safety is known as
a. job instruction training.
b. basic skills training.
c. on-the-job training.
d. coaching and mentoring.

6 _______ 28. High ranking managers responsible for fostering the ethical climate within their firms are called
a. chief learning officer.
b. chief executive officer
c. chief ethics officer
d. chief training officer

6 _______ 29. An awareness of the varied demographics of the workforce, the challenges of affirmative action, the dynamics of stereotyping, the changing values of the workforce, and the potential competitive payoffs from bringing different people together for a common purpose is known as
a. diversity training.
b. basic skills training.
c. on-the-job training.
d. computer-assisted training.

6 _______ 30. To avoid the pitfalls of substandard diversity training, managers will want to do the following, *except*
a. forge a strategic link.
b. check out consultant qualifications.
c. analyze and review performance appraisal methods.
d. choose training methods carefully.

True/False

Identify the following statements as True or False.

1 _______ 1. As a result of training, employees may be even more ineffective on the job and will not be able to perform other jobs in other areas or at higher levels.

1 _______ 2. The training program of the systems approach involves three phases: needs assessment, program design, and implementation.

1 _______ 3. The last step in needs assessment is identifying the broad forces that can influence training needs.

2 _______ 4. Task analysis involves reviewing the job description and specifications to identify the activities performed in a particular job and the knowledge, skills, and aptitudes (KSAs) needed to perform them.

2 _______ 5. Person analysis involves determining which employees require training and, equally important, which do not.

2 _______ 6. Most employees are motivated by certain common needs and are similar in the relative importance of these needs at any given time.

3 _______ 7. The value of goal setting for focusing and motivating behavior extends into training.

3 _______ 8. Even modeling the wrong behavior can be helpful if it shows trainees what not to do and if the appropriate behavior is then demonstrated.

3 _______ 9. Feedback is simply the feeling of accomplishment that follows successful performance of training.

4 _______ 10. The success of any training effort will depend in large part on the teaching skills and personal characteristics of those responsible for conducting the training.

4 _______ 11. All types of organizations use on-the-job training (OJT), and it is one of the most efficiently implemented training methods.

4 _______ 12. With apprenticeship training, thorough instruction and experience, both on and off the job, in the practical and theoretical aspects of the work are given to individuals entering the industry.

4 _______ 13. The term "cooperative training" is typically used in connection with high school and college programs that incorporate part-time or full-time job experiences.

4 _______ 14. The programmed training method lends itself particularly to training in areas where information can be presented in lectures, demonstrations, films, and videotapes or through computer instruction.

4 _______ 15. While programmed instruction increases the amount an individual learns, it typically decreases the speed at which he or she learns.

4 _______ 16. By presenting managers with the opportunities to perform under pressure and to learn from their mistakes, on-the-job development experiences are some of the most powerful and commonly used techniques.

4 _______ 17. Seminars and conferences, unlike classroom instruction, are useful for bringing groups of people together for training and development.

5 _______ 18. Testing knowledge and skills before beginning a training program gives a baseline standard on trainees that can be measured again after training to determine improvement.

5 _______ 19. Basic-skills training is the formal process of familiarizing new employees with the organization, their jobs, and their work units.

5 _______ 20. To evaluate benchmarking standards, the late W. Edwards Deming's classic four-step process for needs assessment advocates that managers plan, do, check, and act.

5 _______ 21. To use benchmarking successfully in training, managers must clearly define the measures of competency and performance and must objectively assess the current situation and identify areas of improvement.

6 _______ 22. To get new employees off to a good start, organizations generally offer a formal orientation program.

6 _______ 23. The supervisor has the least important role in the orientation program.

6 _______ 24. While there are different possible approaches to ensuring that employees have basic skills, the establishment of in-house basic skills programs has decreased in favor.

6 _______ 25. Organizations that have been successful with diversity training realize that it is a long-term process that requires the highest level of skill.

Matching

Match each term with the proper definition.

Terms

a. apprenticeship training
b. behavior modeling
c. behavior modification
d. benchmarking
e. competency assessment
f. cooperative training
g. cross-training
h. e-learning
i. instructional objectives
j. internship programs
k. on-the-job training (OJT)
l. organization analysis
m. orientation
n. person analysis
o. blended learning
p. chief ethics officer
q. task analysis
r. transfer of training
s. chief learning officer
t. just-in time training
u. learning management system

Definitions

_______ 1. an examination of the environment, strategies, and resources of the organization to determine where training emphasis should be placed

_______ 2. programs jointly sponsored by colleges, universities, and other organizations that offer students the opportunity to gain real-life experience while allowing them to find out how they will perform in an organization

_______ 3. formal process of familiarizing new employees with the organization, their jobs, and their work units

_______ 4. training program that combines practical on-the-job experience with formal educational classes

_______ 5. effective application of principles to what is required on the job

_______ 6. system of training in which a worker entering the skilled trades is given thorough instruction and experience, both on and off the job, in the practical and theoretical aspects of the work

_______ 7. determines which employees require training and which do not

_______ 8. process of determining what the content of a training program should be on the basis of a study of the tasks or duties involved in the job

_______ 9. desired outcomes of a training program

_______ 10. approach that demonstrates desired behavior and gives trainees the chance to practice and role-play those behaviors and receive feedback

_______ 11. method by which employees are given hands-on experience with instructions from their supervisor or other trainer

_______ 12. process of measuring an organization's own services and practices against the recognized industry leaders in order to identify areas for improvement

_______ 13. analysis of the sets of skills and knowledge needed for decision-oriented and knowledge-intensive jobs

_______ 14. technique that operates on the principle that behavior that is rewarded or positively reinforced will be exhibited more frequently in the future, whereas behavior that is penalized or unrewarded will decrease in frequency

_______ 15. the process of training employees to do multiple jobs within the organization

_______ 16. audiovisual, programmed, and computer-oriented training methods

_______ 17. training methods that use multiple techniques

_______ 18. high ranking manager responsible for fostering the ethical climate within the firm

_______ 19. top company executive responsible for making certain that training is timely and focused on the firm's top strategic issues

_______ 20. providing training opportunities to employees where and when they need them

_______ 21. combination of e-learning, employee assessment tools, and other training functions

Internet Exercises

How can companies tell whether on-the-job training has been worth it?
http://www.findarticles.com/p/articles/mi_m0DTI/is_10_31/ai_n6335227.

What is an internship and why should a student do one?
http://careerservices.class.umn.edu/students/internships.html

How to Begin Orientation and Training

1. How would you inquire about and prepare for orientation and training programs? During the interview, you should inquire about the orientation and training you will receive once hired. To minimize anxiety, an orientation program should address the job description, the people or employees you are expected to work with, and the crossover between departments. A checklist will help you focus on information relevant to performance of the job. Ask questions such as the following about the training programs offered to new employees: What are the objectives of the training program? What type of training program is used? How is the training program evaluated? How long is the training program? How often are individuals retrained? Is retraining continuous?

2. As a student, how important is it to know how to benefit from an organization's orientation and training program? A new recruit should work with the Human Resources Department and learn everything about the organization's policies, procedures, and rules. Ask for an occupational manual to learn everything you can about the new job.

SOLUTIONS

Multiple Choice:	True/False:	Matching:
1. b	1. False	1. l
2. a	2. False	2. j
3. a	3. False	3. m
4. c	4. True	4. f
5. d	5. True	5. r
6. d	6. False	6. a
7. a	7. True	7. n
8. d	8. True	8. q
9. c	9. False	9. i

10. a
11. a
12. b
13. b
14. b
15. d
16. d
17. d
18. b
19. a
20. d
21. b
22. d
23. b
24. d
25. c
26. d
27. b
28. c
29. a
30. c

10. True
11. False
12. True
13. True
14. False
15. False
16. True
17. False
18. True
19. False
20. True
21. True
22. True
23. False
24. False
25. True

10. b
11. k
12. d
13. e
14. c
15. g
16. h
17. o
18. p
19. s
20. t
21. u

False Statements Made True

1. As a result of training, employees may be even more **effective** on the job and **may** be able to perform other jobs in other areas or at higher levels.
2. The training program of the systems approach involves **four** phases: needs assessment, program design, implementation, **and evaluation**.
3. The **first** step in needs assessment is identifying the broad forces that can influence training needs.
6. **While** most employees are motivated by certain common needs, they **differ from one another** in the relative importance of these needs at any given time.
9. **Reinforcement** is simply the feeling of accomplishment that follows successful performance of training.
11. All types of organizations use on-the-job training (OJT); **however,** it is one of the most **poorly** implemented training methods.
14. The **classroom** training method lends itself particularly to training in areas where information can be presented in lectures, demonstrations, films, and videotapes or through computer instruction.
15. While programmed instruction **may not increase** the amount an individual learns, it typically **increases** the speed at which he or she learns.

17. Seminars and conferences, **like** classroom instruction, are useful for bringing groups of people together for training and development.
19. **Orientation** is the formal process of familiarizing new employees with the organization, their jobs, and their work units.
23. The supervisor has the **most** important role in the orientation program.
24. While there are different possible approaches to ensuring that employees have basic skills, the establishment of in-house basic skills programs has **come increasingly into** favor.

CHAPTER

8

APPRAISING AND IMPROVING PERFORMANCE

A major function of human resources management is the appraisal and improvement of employee performance. In establishing a performance appraisal program, managers should give careful attention to its objectives and to the criteria against which employees are to be evaluated. Court decisions have emphasized the importance of having carefully defined and measurable criteria. Newer methods and techniques for appraisal are replacing some of the older methods that are more subject to errors. The methods used should be consistent with the objectives of appraisal in the particular organization. Through interviews, managers can give information from the appraisal to subordinates and make plans for improving performance.

LEARNING OBJECTIVES

After studying this chapter, you should be able to

1 Explain the purposes of performance appraisals and the reasons they can sometimes fail. Identify the characteristics of an effective appraisal program.

2 Describe the different sources of appraisal information.

3 Explain the various methods used for performance evaluation.

4 Outline the characteristics of an effective performance appraisal interview.

CHAPTER SUMMARY RELATING TO LEARNING OBJECTIVES

1 Performance appraisal programs serve many purposes, but in general those purposes can be clustered into two categories: administrative and developmental. The administrative purposes include decisions about who will be promoted, transferred, or laid off. Appraisals are can also conducted in order to make compensation decisions. Developmental decisions include those related to improving and enhancing an individual's capabilities. These include identifying a person's strengths and weaknesses, eliminating external performance obstacles, and establishing training needs.

Some human resource experts and firms believe performance appraisals are ineffective. In other organizations, performance appraisals are seen as a necessary evil. Managers frequently avoid conducting appraisals because they dislike passing judgment on people. Furthermore, if managers are not adequately trained, subjectivity and organizational politics can distort employee reviews. The do not develop good feedback skills and are often not prepared to conduct an appraisal. As a consequence, the appraisal is done begrudgingly once a year and then forgotten. The ultimate success or failure of a performance appraisal program depends on the philosophy underlying it, its connection with the firm's business goals, and the attitudes and skills of those responsible for its administration.

2 To determine the contributions of each individual, it is necessary to have a formal appraisal program with clearly stated objectives. Carefully defined performance standards that are reliable, strategically relevant, and free from either criterion deficiency or contamination are essential foundations for evaluation. Appraisal systems must also comply with the law and, like selections tests, be valid and reliable. Appraisals should be treated with the same concerns for validity as are selection tests. For example, ratings must be job related, employees must understand their performance standards in advance, appraisers must be able to observe job performance, appraisers must be trained, feedback must be given, and an appeals procedure must be established. Some companies now hold calibration meetings to ensure their managers are accurately rating employees. Using multiple raters is frequently a good idea because different individuals see different facets of an employee's performance. The supervisor, for example, has legitimate authority over an employee and is in a good position to discern whether he or she is contributing to the goals of the organization. Peers and team members, on the other hand, often have an unfiltered view of an employee's work activity, particularly related to issues such as cooperation and dependability. Subordinates often provide good information about whether an employee is facilitating their work, and customers (both internal and external) can convey the extent to which an employee adds value and meets their requirements. Self-appraisal is useful, if for no other reason than it encourages employees to think about their strengths, weaknesses, and future goals. An increasing number of organizations are using multiple raters—or 360-degree appraisal—to get a more comprehensive picture of employee performance. Regardless of the source of

appraisal information, appraisers should be thoroughly trained in the particular methods they will use in evaluating their subordinates. Participation in developing rating scales, such as behaviorally anchored rating scales (BARS), automatically provides such training.

3 Several methods can be used for performance appraisal. These include trait approaches (such as graphic rating scales, mixed-standard scales, forced-choice forms, and essays), behavioral methods (such as critical incidents ratings, checklists, BARS, and BOS), and results methods (MBO). The choice of method depends on the purpose of the appraisal. Trait appraisals are simple to develop and complete, but they have problems of subjectivity and are not useful for feedback. Behavioral methods provide more specific information for giving feedback but can be time-consuming and costly to develop. Results appraisals are more objective and can link individual performance to the organization as a whole, but they may encourage a short-term perspective (e.g., annual goals) and may not include subtle yet important aspects of performance.

4 The degree to which the performance appraisal program benefits an organization and its members is directly related to the quality of the appraisal interviews that are conducted. Interviewing skills are best developed through instruction and supervised practice. Although there are various approaches to the interview, research suggests that employee participation and goal setting lead to higher satisfaction and improved performance. Discussing problems, showing support, minimizing criticism, and rewarding effective performance are also beneficial practices. During the interview, performance deficiencies can be discussed and plans for improvement can be made.

REVIEW QUESTIONS

Multiple Choice

Choose the letter of the word or phrase that best completes each statement.

1 _______ 1. A process typically delivered annually by a supervisor to a subordinate designed to help employees understand their roles, objectives, expectations, and performance success is
   a. job evaluation.
   b. job analysis.
   c. job specification.
   d. performance appraisal.

1 _______ 2. The process of creating a work environment in which people can perform to the best of their ability is
   a. performance appraisal.
   b. management by objectives.
   c. performance management.
   d. benchmarking.

1 _______ 3. One of the objectives of supervisors in observing the day-to-day performance of their employees is to develop a(n)
   a. annual, or semiannual, performance review.
   b. job specification.
   c. critical incident.
   d. error of central tendency.

1 _______ 4. Before any performance appraisal is conducted, the standards by which performance is to be evaluated should be clearly defined and
   a. communicated to the employee.
   b. only then should training commence.
   c. the error of central tendency communicated.
   d. the halo error communicated.

1 _______ 5. The following basic considerations should be included in establishing performance standards, *except*
   a. strategic relevance.
   b. criterion deficiency.
   c. criterion contamination.
   d. inconsistent performance.

1 _______ 6. When performance standards focus on a single criterion to the exclusion of other important but less quantifiable performance dimensions, the appraisal system is said to suffer from
   a. leniency error.
   b. strictness error.
   c. criterion deficiency.
   d. errors of central tendency.

1 _______ 7. The measure of stability or consistency of a standard, or the extent to which individuals tend to maintain a certain level of performance over time, is called
a. validity.
b. reliability.
c. critical incidence.
d. graphic rating.

1 _______ 8. The measure that permits managers to specify and communicate precise information to employees regarding quality and quantity of output is called
a. reliability.
b. halo error.
c. graphic rating.
d. performance standards.

1 _______ 9. A process whereby managers meet to discuss the performance of individual employees to ensure their employee appraisal are in line with one another is called
a. reliability.
b. halo error.
c. graphic rating.
d. calibration.

2 _______ 10. Having appraisals reviewed by a supervisor's superior reduces the chance of
a. validity.
b. biased evaluations.
c. peer appraisals.
d. performance.

2 _______ 11. The appraisal in which individuals of equal rank who work together are increasingly asked to evaluate each other is called
a. team appraisal.
b. 360-degree feedback.
c. peer appraisal.
d. customer appraisal.

2 _______ 12. A company's interest in team appraisals is frequently driven by its commitment to
a. total quality management.
b. management by objectives.
c. strictness and leniency errors.
d. central tendency.

2 _______ 13. The process that is intended to provide employees with as accurate a view of their performance as possible by getting input from others is called
a. central tendency.
b. critical incident.
c. an assessment center.
d. 360-degree feedback.

2 _______ 14. The opposite of horn error is
a. halo error.
b. error of central tendency.
c. strictness and leniency error.
d. recency error.

2 _______ 15. Raters who are reluctant to assign either extremely high or extremely low ratings commit the
a. halo error.
b. error of central tendency.
c. strictness and leniency error.
d. recency error.

2 _______ 16. When the appraisal is based largely on the employee's current behavior, good or bad, the rater has committed the
a. error of central tendency.
b. recency error.
c. contrast error.
d. leniency or strictness error.

2 _______ 17. When an employee's evaluation is biased either upward or downward because of the performance of another employee evaluated previously, the rater is committing a(n)
a. error of central tendency.
b. recency error.
c. contrast error.
d. leniency or strictness error.

3 _______ 18. Performance appraisal methods can be classified as
a. measuring traits.
b. measuring behaviors.
c. measuring results.
d. all of the above.

3 _______ 19. A method of performance appraisal that is designed to measure the extent to which an employee possesses certain characteristics is called the
a. forced-choice method.
b. trait method.
c. critical incident method.
d. graphic rating-scale method.

3 _______ 20. The performance appraisal method that requires the rater to choose from statements, often in pairs, that appear equally favorable or equally unfavorable is the
a. forced-choice method.
b. essay method.
c. graphic rating-scale method.
d. mixed-standard scale method.

3 _______ 21. A performance appraisal in which the appraiser is required to compose a statement that best describes the employee being appraised is the
a. critical incident method.
b. forced-choice method.
c. mixed-standard scale.
d. essay method.

3 _______ 22. An unusual event that denotes superior or inferior employee performance in some part of the job is
a. a critical incident.
b. management by objectives.
c. a halo error.
d. an essay method.

3 ______ 23. Rather than looking at the traits of employees or the behaviors they exhibit on the job, many organizations evaluate
a. employee personalities.
b. employee attributes.
c. employee accomplishments.
d. employee turnover.

3 ______ 24. Which of the following is a behavioral method of performance appraisal?
a. forced-choice method.
b. essay method.
c. critical incident method.
d. graphic rating-scale method.

3 ______ 25. A system involving a cycle that begins with setting the organization's common goals and objectives and ultimately returns to that step is called
a. management by objectives.
b. the critical incident method.
c. the forced-choice method.
d. the essay method.

3 ______ 26. The choice of method for a performance appraisal should be based largely on the
a. critical incident.
b. purpose of the appraisal.
c. employee turnover.
d. personality of the raters.

3 ______ 27. Which method can be used to appraise individual employees, teams, business units, and the corporation itself?
a. the balanced scorecard.
b. the critical incident method.
c. the forced-choice method.
d. the essay method.

4 ______ 28. A format that attempts to give feedback to employees on their job performance and on planning for their future development is a(n)
a. job description.
b. critical incident.
c. halo error.
d. appraisal interview.

4 ________ 29. Norman R. F. Maier analyzes the cause-and-effect relationships in the following types of appraisal interviews, *except*
a. tell-and-sell.
b. tell-and-listen.
c. problem solving.
d. self-assessment.

4 ________ 30. The core purpose of the performance appraisal interview is to
a. express appreciation to the employees.
b. initiate a dialogue that will help an employee improve his or her performance.
c. Figure out why an employee behaves in a certain way
d. tell the employees where all he or she needs to improve

True/False

Identify the following statements as True or False.

1 ________ 1. From the standpoint of individual development, appraisal does not provide the feedback essential for determining strengths and weaknesses as well as improving performance.

1 ________ 2. If the support of top management is encouraged, the performance appraisal system still should be utilized without employee support.

1 ________ 3. An important principle of performance appraisal is continual feedback, and employee coaching must be a positive daily activity.

1 ________ 4. By addressing employee concerns during the planning stage of the performance appraisal process, the organization will help the appraisal program to succeed in reaching its goals.

1 ________ 5. Organizational politics create fairness or equity in employee performance appraisals.

1 ________ 6. When performance standards are properly established, they do not help translate organizational goals and objectives into job requirements that convey acceptable and unacceptable levels of performance to employees.

1 ________ 7. Performance standards will permit managers to specify and communicate imprecise information to employees regarding quality and quantity of output.

1 _______ 8. Performance standards, when written, should be defined in quantifiable and measurable terms.

1 _______ 9. As the courts have made clear, a central issue in performance appraisal systems is to have carefully defined and measurable performance standards.

1 _______ 10. Employers might face legal challenges to their appraisal systems when appraisals indicate acceptable or above-average performance but employees are passed over for promotion, disciplined for poor performance, or discharged.

1 _______ 11. To comply with the legal requirements of performance appraisals, employers must ensure that managers and supervisors document appraisals and reasons for subsequent human resources management actions.

2 _______ 12. Self-appraisal is detrimental when managers seek to increase an employee's involvement in the review process.

2 _______ 13. Self-appraisals may be best for administrative decisions rather than developmental purposes.

2 _______ 14. Subordinate appraisals give employees power over their bosses, making managers hesitant to endorse such a system, particularly when it might be used as a basis for compensation decisions.

2 _______ 15. One advantage of peer appraisals is the belief that they furnish less accurate and invalid information than appraisals by superiors.

2 _______ 16. Although 360-degree feedback can be useful for both developmental and administrative purposes, most companies start with an exclusive focus on development.

2 _______ 17. A weakness of many performance appraisal programs is that managers and supervisors are not adequately trained for the appraisal task and provide little meaningful feedback to subordinates.

2 _______ 18. Managers who give higher ratings because they believe an employee is "showing improvement" may unwittingly be committing recency error.

3 _______ 19. The fact that trait methods are the least popular method of performance appraisal is due in large part to the ease with which they are developed.

3 _______ 20. The mixed-standard scale of performance appraisal method is a modification of the basic behavior observation scale.

3 _______ 21. A major limitation of the essay method of performance appraisals

is that composing an essay that attempts to cover all of an employee's essential characteristics is a very time-consuming task.

3 _______ 22. One of the potential advantages of a trait-oriented performance appraisal system is that traits tend to be subjective.

4 _______ 23. The appraisal interview gives a manager the opportunity to discuss a subordinate's performance record and to explore areas of possible improvement and growth.

4 _______ 24. Managers should assume that only one type of appraisal interview is appropriate for every review session.

4 _______ 25. The core purpose of a performance appraisal interview is to initiate a dialogue that will help an employee improve her or his performance.

Matching

Match each term with the proper definition.

Terms

a. behavior observation scale (BOS)
b. behaviorally anchored rating scale
c. contrast error
d. critical incident
e. customer appraisal
f. error of central tendency
g. essay method
h. forced-choice method
i. graphic rating-scale method
j. leniency or strictness error
k. management by objectives (MBO)
l. manager and/or supervisor appraisal
m. mixed-standard scale method
n. peer appraisal
o. performance appraisal
p. performance management
q. recency error
r. self-appraisal
s. similar-to-me error
t. subordinate appraisal
u. team appraisal
v. calibration

Definitions

_______ 1. a process typically delivered annually by a supervisor to a subordinate, designed to help employees understand their roles, objectives, expectations, and performance success

_______ 2. philosophy of management that rates performance on the basis of employee achievement of goals set by the mutual agreement of employee and manager

_______ 3. performance appraisal, based on TQM concepts, that recognizes team accomplishment rather than individual performance

_______ 4. a behavioral approach to performance appraisal that measures the frequency of observed behavior

_______ 5. a trait approach to performance appraisal that requires the rater to compose a statement describing employee behavior

_______ 6. performance appraisal that, like team appraisal, is based on TQM concepts and seeks evaluation from both external and internal customers

_______ 7. performance-rating error in which an employee's evaluation is biased either upward or downward because of comparison with another employee just previously evaluated

_______ 8. performance-rating error in which an appraiser inflates the evaluation of an employee because of a mutual personal connection

_______ 9. a trait approach to performance appraisal whereby each employee is rated according to a scale of characteristics

_______ 10. performance appraisal done by one's fellow employees that are generally compiled into a single profile to be used in the performance interview conducted by the employee's manager

_______ 11. unusual event that denotes superior or inferior employee performance in some part of the job

_______ 12. performance appraisal of a superior by an employee, which is more appropriate for developmental than for administrative purposes

_______ 13. performance-rating error in which all employees are rated about average

_______ 14. a trait approach to performance appraisal similar to other scale methods but based on comparison with (better than, equal to, or worse than) a standard

_______ 15. a behavioral approach to performance appraisal that consists of a series of vertical scales, one for each important dimension of job performance

_______ 16. performance appraisal done by the employee being evaluated, generally on an appraisal form completed by the employee prior to the performance interview

_______ 17. performance appraisal done by an employee's manager and often reviewed by a manager one level higher

_______ 18. a trait approach to performance appraisal that requires the rater to choose from statements designed to distinguish between successful and unsuccessful performance

_______ 19. performance-rating error in which the appraiser tends to give employees either unusually high or unusually low ratings

_______ 20. the process of creating a work environment in which people can perform to the best of their abilities

_______ 21. performance-rating error in which the appraisal is based largely on the employee's most recent behavior rather than on behavior throughout the appraisal period

_______ 22. a process whereby managers meet to discuss the performance of individual employees to ensure their employee appraisal are in line with one another.

Internet Exercises

What is the manager's primary responsibility toward employees?
http://www.findarticles.com/p/articles/mi_m0KJI/is_2_117/ai_n12414578.

What is the role of a team leader in managing subordinates?
http://www.findarticles.com/p/articles/mi_qa3616?is_200304/ai_n9173768.

How to Prepare for a Performance Appraisal Interview

You should understand the objective of performance appraisal. Employees need feedback to understand how secure they are within the organization. It is important that the employee knows the work activity required to perform her or his job. A performance appraisal interview will accomplish such objectives.

A performance appraisal is conducted to assess the performance of the individual in his or her job operations. There are different performance appraisal methods and different means to accomplish this activity. Traditionally, a supervisor evaluates the performance of the employee. There are also peer-based, self-directed, and customer-based methods of doing performance appraisals.

In the traditional method of interviewing, the supervisor should have a thorough understanding of the employee's job description. In addition, the performance appraisal should be put in writing and taken into the interview with the supervisor. The appraisal should be used as a basis for merit reviews and should be signed at the end of the interview to indicate that the supervisor has reviewed the performance appraisal with the employee. Finally, there should be an appeal process if the employee disagrees with the appraisal.

SOLUTIONS

Multiple Choice:	True/False:	Matching:
1. d	1. False	1. o
2. c	2. False	2. k
3. a	3. True	3. u
4. a	4. True	4. a
5. d	5. False	5. g
6. c	6. False	6. e
7. b	7. False	7. c
8. d	8. True	8. s
9. d	9. True	9. i
10. b	10. True	10. n
11. c	11. True	11. d
12. a	12. False	12. t
13. d	13. False	13. f
14. a	14. True	14. m
15. b	15. False	15. b
16. b	16. True	16. r
17. c	17. True	17. l
18. d	18. True	18. h
19. b	19. False	19. j
20. a	20. False	20. p
21. d	21. True	21. q
22. a	22. False	22. v
23. c	23. True	
24. c	24. False	
25. a	25. True	
26. b		
27. a		
28. d		
29. d		
30. b		

False Statements Made True

1. From the standpoint of individual development, appraisal **provides** the feedback essential for determining strengths and weaknesses as well as improving performance.
2. If the support of top management is encouraged, the performance appraisal system **will not be successful** without employee support.

5. Organizational politics **can introduce a bias even in fairly administered** employee performance appraisals.
6. When performance standards are properly established, they **help** translate organizational goals and objectives into job requirements that convey acceptable and unacceptable levels of performance to employees.
7. Performance standards will permit managers to specify and communicate **precise** information to employees regarding quality and quantity of output.
12. Self-appraisal is **beneficial** when managers seek to increase an employee's involvement in the review process.
13. Self-appraisals may be best for **developmental purposes** rather than **administrative decisions**.
15. One advantage of peer appraisals is the belief that they furnish **more** accurate and **valid** information than appraisals by superiors.
19. The fact that trait methods are the **most** popular method of performance appraisal is due in large part to the ease with which they are developed.
20. The mixed-standard scale of performance appraisal method is a modification of the basic **rating-scale method**.
22. One of the potential **drawbacks** of a trait-oriented performance appraisal system is that traits tend to be subjective.
24. Managers should **not** assume that only one type of appraisal interview is appropriate for every review session.

PART FOUR

Implementing Compensation and Security

PART FOUR

Implementing Compensation and

[illegible] COMPENSATION

[illegible] psychological rewards from their jobs [illegible] the compensation they receive. [illegible] in terms of the job's value to the organization and [illegible] receive. The purchasing power of workers' salaries must be [illegible] to accommodate rises in the cost of living. In addition, [illegible] must be consistent with the terms of the labor agreement [illegible] state and federal regulations [illegible] pay compression, and low-wage earners and [illegible] compensation.

[illegible]

[illegible] grades and [illegible]

[illegible]

[illegible] compensation [illegible]

CHAPTER 9

MANAGING COMPENSATION

Employees seek various psychological rewards from their jobs, but this does not diminish the importance of the compensation they receive. It is essential that this compensation be equitable in terms of the job's value to the organization and in relation to the pay other employees receive. The purchasing power of workers' salaries must be adjusted upward periodically to accommodate rises in the cost of living. In addition, compensation payments must be consistent with the terms of the labor agreement, where one exists, and with state and federal regulations governing it. Issues of equal pay for comparable worth, pay compression, and low wage budgets are emerging issues in the field of management compensation.

LEARNING OBJECTIVES

After studying this chapter, you should be able to

1. Explain employer concerns in developing a strategic compensation program.
2. Indicate the various factors that influence the setting of wages.
3. Differentiate the mechanics of each of the major job evaluation systems.
4. Explain the purpose of a wage survey.
5. Define the wage curve, pay grades, and rate ranges as parts of the compensation structure.
6. Identify the major provisions of the federal laws affecting compensation.
7. Discuss the current issues of equal pay for comparable worth, pay compression, and low wage budgets.

CHAPTER SUMMARY RELATING TO LEARNING OBJECTIVES

1 Establishing compensation programs requires both large and small organizations to consider specific goals—employee retention, compensation distribution, and adherence to a budget, for instance. Compensation must reward employees for past efforts (pay-for-performance) while motivating employees' future performance. Internal and external equity of the pay program affects employees' concepts of fairness. Organizations must balance each of these concerns while still remaining competitive. The ability to attract qualified employees while controlling labor costs is a major factor in allowing organizations to remain viable in the domestic or international market.

2 The basis on which compensation payments are determined, and the way they are administered, can significantly affect employee productivity and the achievement of organizational goals. Internal influences include the employer's compensation policy, the worth of the job, the performance of the employee, and the employer's ability to pay. External factors influencing wage rates include labor market conditions, area wage rates, cost of living, the outcomes of collective bargaining, and legal requirements.

3 Organizations use one of four basic job evaluation techniques to determine the relative worth of jobs. The job ranking system arranges jobs in numerical order on the basis of the importance of the job's duties and responsibilities to the organization. The job classification system slots jobs into preestablished grades. Higher-rated grades will require more responsibilities, working conditions, and job duties. The point system of job evaluation uses a point scheme based on the compensable job factors of skill, effort, responsibility, and working conditions. The more compensable factors a job possesses, the more points are assigned to it. Jobs with higher accumulated points are considered more valuable to the organization. The work valuation system evaluates jobs based upon their value relative to organizational goals—financing, customer service, and so on—and the jobs' contribution to organizational success.

4 Wage surveys determine the external equity of jobs. Data obtained from surveys will facilitate establishing the organization's wage policy while ensuring that the employer does not pay more, or less, than needed for jobs in the relevant labor market.

5 The wage structure is composed of the wage curve, pay grades, and rate ranges. The wage curve depicts graphically the pay rates assigned to jobs within each pay grade. Pay grades represent the grouping of similar jobs on the basis of their relative worth. Each pay grade will include a rate range. Rate ranges will have a midpoint and minimum and maximum pay rates for all jobs in the pay grade.

6 Both the Davis-Bacon Act and the Walsh-Healy Act are prevailing wage statutes. These laws require government contractors to pay wages normally based on the union scale in the employer's operating area. The Walsh-Healy Act also requires payment of one and one-half times the regular pay for hours over eight per day or forty per week. The Fair Labor Standards Act contains provisions covering the federal minimum wage, hours worked, and child labor.

7 The concept of comparable worth seeks to overcome the fact that jobs held by women are compensated at a lower rate than those performed by men. This happens even though both types of jobs may contribute equally to organizational productivity. Low wage increases are prominent compensation strategies as employers seek to hold pay down to adjust to competitive challenges. Wage-rate compression is the narrowing of pay between new, or less experienced employees and experienced senior employees. The primary cause of the problem is the high salaries paid to new employees. Hourly employees and their managers may experience pay compression when the salary spread between the two groups is low.

REVIEW QUESTIONS

Multiple Choice

Choose the letter of the word or phrase that best completes each statement.

1 ________ 1. Linking compensation to organizational objectives, the pay-for-performance standard, and the motivating value of compensation are aspects of
   a. job enlargement.
   b. strategic compensation planning.
   c. job enrichment.
   d. employee empowerment.

1 ________ 2. A program in which components of the compensation package create value for the organization and its employees is called
   a. value-added compensation.
   b. pay-for-performance standard.
   c. pay equity.
   d. competence-based pay.

1 _______ 3. Equity theory is also referred to as
a. value-added theory.
b. pay-for-performance standard.
c. distributive fairness.
d. competence-based theory.

1 _______ 4. A wide range of compensation options, including merit-based pay, bonuses, salary commissions, job and pay banding, team/group incentives, and various gainsharing programs, is called
a. job evaluation.
b. performance appraisal.
c. pay-for-performance.
d. management by objectives.

1 _______ 5. When employees believe that the wage rates for their jobs approximate the job's worth to the organization, compensation policies are considered to be
a. mixed combinations.
b. externally equitable.
c. paired comparisons.
d. internally equitable.

1 _______ 6. The situation that exists when an organization is paying wages that are relatively equal to what other employers are paying for similar types of work is known as
a. external pay equity.
b. comparable worth.
c. internal pay equity.
d. equity theory of motivation.

1 _______ 7. The theory that predicts how one's level of motivation depends on the attractiveness of the rewards sought and the probability of obtaining those rewards is the
a. two-factor theory of motivation.
b. equity theory of motivation.
c. expectancy theory of motivation.
d. needs hierarchy theory.

1 _______ 8. A system of pay in which employees are paid according to the number of units they produce is
a. hourly work.
b. salary.
c. piecework.
d. real wages.

2 _______ 9. An internal factor affecting the wage mix is
a. worth of job.
b. job evaluation programs.
c. job analysis programs.
d. incentive programs.

2 _______ 10. An external factor affecting the wage mix is
a. cost of living.
b. job evaluation programs.
c. job analysis programs.
d. incentive programs.

2 _______ 11. In both hourly and salary jobs, differences in employee performance can be recognized and rewarded through promotion and with various
a. child care programs.
b. job evaluation programs.
c. job analysis programs.
d. incentive programs.

2 _______ 12. A means of wage payment that can be affected by earned profits and other financial resources available to employers is a(n)
a. employee worth system.
b. pay level.
c. critical incident.
d. job evaluation program.

2 _______ 13. Due to inflation, compensation rates have been adjusted upward periodically to help employees maintain their
a. comparable worth.
b. job evaluation.
c. purchasing power.
d. noneconomic benefits.

3 _______ 14. In job evaluation, jobs are classified and grouped according to a series of predetermined grades in the
a. job classification system.
b. job ranking method.
c. point system.
d. factor comparison method.

3 _______ 15. A quantitative job evaluation procedure that determines the relative value of a job by the total points assigned to it is the
a. points system.
b. factor comparison method.
c. job classification system.
d. job ranking system.

3 _______ 16. The point system of job evaluation requires the use of a
a. job specification.
b. job description.
c. job analysis.
d. points manual.

3 _______ 17. A job evaluation system that has been developed specifically to evaluate executive, managerial, and professional positions is the
a. essay method.
b. forced-choice method.
c. critical incidents method.
d. Hay profile method.

3 _______ 18. A job evaluation system that uses knowledge, mental activity, and accountability to evaluate positions is the
a. essay method.
b. forced-choice method.
c. critical incidents method.
d. Hay profile method.

4 _______ 19. Job evaluation systems provide for internal equity and serve as the basis for
a. wage-rate determination.
b. performance appraisal.
c. job analysis.
d. comparable worth issues.

4 _______ 20. A major national publisher of wage and salary data is the
a. Chamber of Commerce.
b. Bureau of Labor Statistics.
c. Internal Revenue Service.
d. Local Employer Association.

5 _______ 21. The relationship between the relative worth of employees' jobs and their wage rates can be represented by means of a(n)
a. escalator clause.
b. comparable worth system.
c. wage curve.
d. job ranking system.

5 _______ 22. Wages paid above the range maximum are called
a. competence-based pay.
b. comparable worth.
c. red circle rates.
d. wage-rate compression.

5 _______ 23. The method that compensates employees for the different skills or increased knowledge they possess rather than for the job they hold in a designated job category is known as
a. broadbanding.
b. competence-based pay.
c. job enlargement.
d. pay-for-performance.

5 _______ 24. The concept in which organizations adopt a competence-based pay system to structure their compensation payments to employees is
a. broadbanding.
b. external pay equity.
c. job enrichment.
d. job enlargement.

6 _______ 25. The major provisions of the Fair Labor Standards Act include the following, *except*
a. equal pay for equal work.
b. minimum-wage rates.
c. overtime payments.
d. child labor.

6 _______ 26. Which act is also referred to as the Prevailing Wage Law?
a. Equal Pay Act.
b. Davis-Bacon Act.
c. Walsh-Healy Act.
d. Fair Labor Standards Act

7

_______ 27. The concept in which jobs historically held exclusively by men and by women are considered equal in terms of value or worth to the employer is known as
a. sexual harassment.
b. job evaluation.
c. comparable worth.
d. external pay equity.

7

_______ 28. The internal pay-equity concern that results in the reduction of differences between job classes is
a. employee empowerment.
b. job enlargement.
c. job specification.
d. wage-rate compression.

7

_______ 29. When wage-rate compression exists, all of the following exist, *except*
a. low employee morale.
b. increased fatigue at work.
c. reduced employee performance.
d. employee theft.

7

_______ 30. Unfavorable effects for employers and society such as increased employee turnover and diminished employee output may be a result of
a. low wages.
b. high wages.
c. real wages.
d. wage-rate compression.

True/False

Identify the following statements as True or False.

1

_______ 1. Pay equity is achieved when the compensation received is unequal to the value of the work performed.

1

_______ 2. Work performed in most private, public, and not-for-profit organizations has traditionally been compensated on a professionally contracted basis.

1 _______ 3. Salaried employees are generally paid the same for each pay period, even though they occasionally may work more hours or fewer than the regular number of hours in a period.

1 _______ 4. Managers and supervisors as well as a large number of white-collar employees are in the nonexempt category of pay structure.

2 _______ 5. Economic conditions and competition faced by employers do not significantly affect the rates they are able to pay.

2 _______ 6. The major external factors that influence wage rates include labor market conditions, area wage rates, cost of living, legal requirements, and the employer's ability to pay.

2 _______ 7. The consumer price index (CPI) is based on prices of food, clothing, shelter, and fuels; transportation fares; charges for medical services; and prices of other goods and services that people buy for day-to-day living.

3 _______ 8. All job evaluation methods require the same consistent degree of managerial judgment.

3 _______ 9. Job ranking can be done by a single individual who has a working knowledge of all jobs; however, it should never be done by a committee composed of management and employee representatives.

3 _______ 10. The basic weakness of the job ranking system is that it does not provide a very refined measure of each job's worth.

3 _______ 11. The principle advantage of the point system job evaluation technique is that it provides a more refined basis for making judgments than either the ranking or classification systems.

3 _______ 12. The cornerstone for work valuation is that work should be valued relative to the business goals of the organization rather than by an internally applied points-factor job evaluation system.

4 _______ 13. Many states conduct wage and salary surveys on either a municipal or county basis and make them available to the Internal Revenue Service.

5 _______ 14. A wage curve may be constructed graphically by preparing a scattergram, which consists of a series of dots that represent the current inflation rates.

5 _______ 15. From an administrative standpoint, it is generally preferable to group jobs into pay grades and to pay all jobs within a particular grade a different rate or rate range.

5 _______ 16. Pay grades are groups of jobs within a particular class that are paid different rates.

5 _______ 17. The final step in setting up a wage structure is to determine the appropriate pay grade into which each job should be placed on the basis of its evaluated worth.

5 _______ 18. Broadbanding uses many traditional salary grades for employee compensation.

6 _______ 19. The three principal federal laws affecting wages are the Davis-Bacon Act, the Walsh-Healy Act, and the Fair Labor Standards Act.

6 _______ 20. Under the Fair Labor Standards Act (FLSA), employers are not required to pay time-and-a-half wages for hours worked in excess of forty hours in any particular week.

6 _______ 21. One of the most significant amendments to the FLSA was the Equal Pay Act passed in 1963.

7 _______ 22. As managers strive to reward employees in a fair manner, they must consider controls over labor costs, legal issues regarding male and female wage payments, and external pay-equity concerns.

7 _______ 23. There are several causes for wage-rate compression, including job analysis, job evaluation, and performance appraisal.

7 _______ 24. Wage-rate compression often occurs when organizations grant pay adjustments for lower-rated jobs without providing commensurate adjustments for occupations at the top of the job hierarchy.

7 _______ 25. Identifying wage-rate compression and its causes is far simpler than implementing organizational policies to alleviate its effects.

Matching

Match each term with the proper definition.

Terms

a. comparable worth
b. competence-based pay
c. consumer price index (CPI)
d. escalator clauses
e. exempt employees
f. Hay profile method
g. hourly work
h. job classification system
i. job evaluation
j. job ranking system
k. nonexempt employees
l. pay equity
m. pay-for-performance
n. pay grades
o. piecework
p. point system
q. real wages
r. red circle rates
s. employee compensation
t. wage and salary survey
u. wage curve
v. wage-rate compression
w. work valuation

Definitions

_______ 1. curve in a scattergram representing the relationship between the relative worth of jobs and their wage rates

_______ 2. quantitative job evaluation procedure that determines the relative value of a job by the total points assigned to it

_______ 3. standard by which managers tie compensation to employee effort and performance

_______ 4. the concept that male and female jobs that are dissimilar but equal in terms of value or worth to the employer should be paid the same

_______ 5. clauses in labor agreements that provide for quarterly cost-of-living adjustment in wages, basing the adjustments on changes in the consumer price index

_______ 6. an employee's perception that compensation received is equal to the value of the work performed

_______ 7. compression of differentials between job classes, particularly the differential between hourly workers and their managers

_______ 8. work paid on an hourly basis

_______ 9. groups of jobs within a particular class that are paid the same rate or rate range

_______ 10. work paid according to the number of units produced

_______ 11. employees not covered by the overtime provisions of the Fair Labor Standards Act

_______ 12. measure of the average change in prices over time in a fixed "market basket" of goods and services

_______ 13. systematic process of determining the relative worth of jobs in order to establish which jobs should be paid more than others within an organization

_______ 14. job evaluation technique using three factors—knowledge, mental activity, and accountability—to evaluate executive and managerial positions

_______ 15. survey of the wages paid to employees of other employers in the surveying organization's relevant labor market

_______ 16. wage increases larger than rises in the consumer price index; that is, the real earning power of wages

_______ 17. simplest and oldest system of job evaluation by which jobs are arrayed on the basis of their relative worth

_______ 18. pay based on an employee's skill level, the variety of skills possessed, or increased job knowledge of the employee

_______ 19. employees covered by the overtime provisions of the Fair Labor Standards Act

_______ 20. system of job evaluation in which jobs are classified and grouped according to a series of predetermined wage grades

_______ 21. all forms of pay and rewards received by employee for the performance of their jobs.

_______ 22. payment rates above the maximum of the pay range

_______ 23. a job evaluation system that seeks to measure a job's worth through its value to the organization

Internet Exercises

Is comparable worth a solution for teachers?
http://www.findarticles.com/p/articles/mi_m0MJG/is_3_3/ai_104835530.

How can the labor force accommodate older workers?
http://www.springerlink.com/content/qjp5p00v83708513/

How to Negotiate a Fair Compensation Package

Research the job market for compensation or salary ranges for a graduating student in the field of business.

Wages and fringe benefits are important issues to present to a prospective employer. To gain access to this type of information, visit the college placement office, local chamber of commerce, library, or Internet.

In negotiating a fair compensation package with an employer, you should understand your economic needs. Offer a salary range rather than an exact amount when a potential employer asks your starting salary requirements. Know your salary objectives and career goals when interviewing with an employer. Following the interview, have questions ready concerning salary objectives and career development opportunities. Utilize previous job experience as a bargaining tool for obtaining a higher starting salary. Apply your marketing knowledge to project a positive image in the interview.

SOLUTIONS

Multiple Choice:	True/False:	Matching:
1. b	1. False	1. u
2. a	2. False	2. p
3. c	3. True	3. m
4. c	4. False	4. a
5. d	5. False	5. d
6. a	6. False	6. l
7. c	7. True	7. v
8. c	8. False	8. g
9. b	9. False	9. n
10. a	10. True	10. o
11. d	11. True	11. e
12. b	12. True	12. c
13. c	13. False	13. i
14. a	14. False	14. f
15. a	15. False	15. t
16. d	16. False	16. q
17. d	17. True	17. j
18. d	18. False	18. b
19. a	19. True	19. k
20. b	20. False	20. h
21. c	21. True	21. s
22. c	22. False	22. r
23. b	23. False	23. w
24. a	24. True	
25. a	25. True	
26. b		
27. c		
28. d		
29. b		
30. a		

False Statements Made True

1. Pay equity is achieved when the compensation received is **equal** to the value of the work performed.
2. Work performed in most private, public, and not-for-profit organizations has traditionally been compensated on **an hourly** basis.
4. Managers and supervisors as well as a large number of white-collar employees are in the **exempt** category of pay structure.
5. Economic conditions and competition faced by employers **significantly** affect the rates they are able to pay.
6. The major external factors that influence wage rates include labor market conditions, area wage rates, cost of living, legal requirements, and **collective bargaining if the employer is unionized.**
8. All job evaluation methods require **varying degrees** of managerial judgment.
9. Job ranking can be done by a single individual who has a working knowledge of all jobs, **or by** a committee composed of management and employee representatives.
13. Many states conduct wage and salary surveys on **local, regional, or national** organizations and make them available to **employers**.
14. A wage curve may be constructed graphically by preparing a scattergram, which consists of a series of dots that represent the current **wage** rates.
15. From an administrative standpoint, it is generally preferable to group jobs into pay grades and to pay all jobs within a particular grade **the same** rate or rate range.
16. Pay grades are groups of jobs within a particular class that are paid **the same rate**.
18. Broadbanding **collapses** many traditional salary grades **into a few wide salary bands**.
20. Under the Fair Labor Standards Act, employers **are** required to pay time-and-a-half wages for hours worked in excess of forty hours in any particular week.
22. As managers strive to reward employees in a fair manner, they must consider controls over labor costs, legal issues regarding male and female wage payments, and **internal** pay-equity concerns.
23. There are several causes for wage-rate compression, including **the granting of union-negotiated across-the-board increases for hourly employees without granting corresponding wage differentials for managerial personnel, and the scarcity of applicants.**

CHAPTER 10

PAY-FOR-PERFORMANCE: INCENTIVE REWARDS

Compensation can be a significant source of motivation if at least part of it is tied directly to the employee's performance. Countless financial incentive systems have been developed over the years to motivate employees who occupy various levels within an organization and who perform different types of duties. Some of these systems have been successful, while others have not. The success of a particular system depends not so much on the formula for determining incentive payments, as on the existence of a favorable climate in which the system can operate. Success also depends on the degree to which the system has been tailored to the needs of the organization where it is to be used. Contributing to this success, furthermore, are the ways in which the system allows employees to participate, psychologically as well as financially, in the organization. A rather new form of compensation—the employee stock ownership plan (ESOP)—can be advantageous to employers and to employees.

LEARNING OBJECTIVES

After studying this chapter, you should be able to

1. Discuss the basic requirements for successful implementation of incentive programs.
2. Identify the types of, and reasons for implementing, individual incentive plans.
3. Explain why merit raises may fail to motivate employees adequately, and discuss ways to increase their motivational value.
4. Indicate the advantage of each of the principal methods used to compensate salespeople.
5. Differentiate how gains may be shared with employees under the Scanlon and Improshare gainsharing systems.
6. Differentiate between profit-sharing plans and explain advantages and disadvantages of these programs.

7 Describe the main types of ESOP plans and discuss the advantages of ESOP to employers and employees.

CHAPTER SUMMARY RELATING TO LEARNING OBJECTIVES

1 The success of an incentive pay plan depends on the organizational climate in which it must operate, employee confidence in it, and its suitability to employee and organizational needs. Importantly, employees must view their incentive pay as being equitable and related to their performance. Performance measures should be quantifiable be easily understood, and bear a demonstrated relationship to organizational performance.

2 Piecework plans pay employees a given rate for each unit satisfactorily completed. Employers implement these plans when output is easily measured and when the production process is fairly standardized. Bonuses are incentive payments above base wages paid on either an individual or a team basis. A bonus is offered to encourage employees to exert greater effort. Standard hour plans establish a standard time for job completion. An incentive is paid for finishing the job in less than the preestablished time. These plans are popular for jobs with a fixed time for completion.

3 Merit raises will not serve to motivate employees when they are seen as entitlements, which occur when these raises are given yearly without regard to changes in employee performance. Merit raises are not motivational when they are given because of seniority or favoritism or when merit budgets are inadequate to sufficiently reward employee performance. To be motivational, merit raises must be such that employees see a clear relationship between pay and performance and the salary increase must be large enough to exceed inflation and higher income taxes.

4 Salespersons may be compensated by a straight salary, a combination of salary and commission, salary plus bonus or a commission only. Paying employees a straight salary allows them to focus on tasks other than sales, such as service and customer goodwill. A straight commission plan causes employees to emphasize sales goals. A combination of salary and commission or bonus provides the advantages of both the straight salary and the straight commission forms of payment.

5 The Scanlon and Improshare gainsharing plans pay bonuses to employees unrelated to profit levels. Each of these plans encourages employees to maximize their performance and cooperation through suggestions offered to improve organizational performance. The Scanlon Plan pays an employee a bonus based on saved labor cost measured against the organization's sales value of production. The Improshare bonus is paid when employees increase production output above a given target level.

6 Profit-sharing plans pay to employees sums of money based on the organization's profits. Cash payments are made to eligible employees at specified times, normally yearly. The primary purpose of profit sharing is to provide employees with additional income through their participation in organizational achievement. Employee commitment to improved productivity, quality, and customer service will contribute to organizational success and, in turn, to their compensation. Profit-sharing plans may not achieve their stated gains when employee performance is unrelated to organizational success or failure. This may occur because of economic conditions, other competition, or environmental conditions. Profit-sharing plans can have a negative effect on employee morale when plans fail to consistently reward employees.

7 With an ESOP, each year the organization contributes stock or cash to buy stock that is then placed in an ESOP trust. The ESOP holds the stock for employees until they either retire or leave the company, at which time the stock is sold back to the company or through a brokerage firm. Employers receive tax benefits for qualified ESOPs; they also hope to receive their employees' commitment to organizational improvement. Employees, however, may lose their retirement income should the company fail or stock prices fall. Another drawback to ESOPs is that they are not guaranteed by any federal agency.

REVIEW QUESTIONS

Multiple Choice

Choose the letter of the word or phrase that best completes each statement.

1 _______ 1. A clear trend in strategic compensation management is the growth of
a. traditional pay plans.
b. incentive plans.
c. obsolescent piece-rate systems.
d. antiquated group incentive systems.

1 _______ 2. Managers believe that employees will assume ownership of their jobs, thereby improving their effort and overall job performance, by meshing
a. traditional pay plans with those of employer associations.
b. compensation with that of the competition.
c. compensation and organizational objectives.
d. compensation programs with those outside the industry.

1 _______ 3. The success of an incentive plan in an organization depends on
   a. employee morale.
   b. treating employees fairly.
   c. harmony between employees and management.
   d. all of the above.

1 _______ 4. Management should never allow incentive payments to be seen as
   a. a bonus.
   b. variable pay.
   c. an entitlement.
   d. a reward.

2 _______ 5. The following impact the organization's choice of incentive pay plans, *except*
   a. technology.
   b. job tasks and duties.
   c. organizational goals.
   d. social orientation.

2 _______ 6. One of the oldest incentive plans is based on
   a. technology.
   b. job tasks and duties.
   c. organizational goals.
   d. piecework.

2 _______ 7. Employees whose production exceeds the standard output receive a higher rate for all of their work than the rate paid to those who do not exceed the standard under a
   a. holidays and vacations system.
   b. differential piece-rate plan.
   c. career curve method.
   d. socialization process.

2 _______ 8. A plan that sets incentive rates on the basis of a predetermined standard time for completing a job is known as the
   a. combined salary and commission plan.
   b. piece-rate incentive plan.
   c. standard hour plan.
   d. street commission plan.

2 _______ 9. An annual payment that is supplemental to the basic wage for employees is a
a. contracted wage.
b. fringe benefit.
c. differential piece rate.
d. bonus.

2 _______ 10. A raise that links an increase in base pay to how successfully an employee performs his or her job is a
a. merit pay program.
b. combined salary and commission plan.
c. piece rate plan.
d. Scanlon Plan.

3 _______ 11. One of the major weaknesses of merit raises lies in increases based on a
a. performance appraisal system.
b. differential piece rate.
c. straight commission plan.
d. competitive benchmarking plan.

3 _______ 12. A method of pay in which employers receive a year-end merit payment that is not added to their base pay is called a
a. combined salary and commission plan.
b. lump-sum merit program.
c. team incentive plan.
d. gainsharing plan.

4 _______ 13. A sales incentive plan that is based on a percentage of sales and provides maximum incentive for the salesperson is the
a. straight salary plan.
b. combined salary and commission plan.
c. Scanlon Plan.
d. straight commission plan.

4 _______ 14. A cash advance which must be paid back as commissions are earned is called a
a. bonus.
b. draw.
c. salary.
d. lump sum.

4

_______ 15. The most widely used sales incentive program is the
a. combined salary and commission plan.
b. straight commission plan.
c. lump-sum bonus.
d. annual bonus.

4

_______ 16. A bonus payment to an executive usually takes the form of
a. increased health benefits and vacation time.
b. increased personal days and sick days.
c. increased holidays and compensatory time.
d. cash or stock.

4

_______ 17. A major long-term incentive for an executive is a(n)
a. piece-rate incentive.
b. stock option.
c. annual bonus.
d. combined salary and commission plan.

4

_______ 18. One means of demonstrating the executive's importance to the organization while giving him or her an incentive to improve performance is a
a. differential piece rate.
b. career curve.
c. perk.
d. straight salary initiative.

4

_______ 19. A grant of stock or stock units at a reduced price with the understanding that the stock not be transferred or sold before a specific employment date is called
a. phantom stock
b. performance units
c. Scanlon Plan.
d. restricted stock.

4

_______ 20. A grant of units equal in value to the fair market value or book value of a share of stock; on a specified day the executive will be paid the appreciation in the value at that time is called
a. phantom stock
b. performance units
c. Scanlon Plan.
d. restricted stock.

5 _______ 21. The Scanlon Plan emphasizes
a. participative management.
b. economic forecasts.
c. supplemental pay benefits.
d. competitive reactions.

5 _______ 22. The type of bonus plan in which employees offer ideas and suggestions to improve productivity in the plant and are then rewarded for their constructive efforts is the
a. annual bonus plan.
b. Scanlon Plan.
c. day-rate plan.
d. combined salary and commission plan.

5 _______ 23. Which of the following is an individual incentive plan?
a. Scanlon Plan.
b. Improshare
c. profit sharing plan
d. piecework

5 _______ 24. Which of the following is a group incentive plan?
a. merit-pay
b. Improshare
c. profit sharing plan
d. piecework

5 _______ 25. Which of the following is an enterprise incentive plan?
a. Scanlon Plan.
b. Improshare
c. profit sharing plan
d. piecework

5 _______ 26. A gainsharing program based upon overall productivity of the work team is called a(n)
a. competition benchmarking program.
b. team incentive plan.
c. earnings-at-risk incentive plan.
d. Improshare plan.

5

_______ 27. Common enterprise incentive plans include
a. profit-sharing.
b. stock options.
c. employee stock ownership plans (ESOPs).
d. all of the above.

6

_______ 28. Any procedure in which an employer pays all regular employees special current or deferred sums based upon the profits of the enterprise is
a. a profit-sharing plan.
b. gainsharing.
c. a Scanlon plan.
d. a piece-rate plan.

6

_______ 29. An incentive plan that gives employees the opportunity to increase their earnings by contributing to the growth of their organization's profits is known as a
a. straight commission plan.
b. straight salary plan.
c. combined salary and commission plan.
d. profit-sharing plan.

7

_______ 30. The type of incentive that may take the form of a stock bonus plan or a leveraged plan is the
a. employee stock ownership plan.
b. performance units
c. Scanlon Plan.
d. combined salary and commission plan.

True/False

Identify the following statements as True or False.

1 _______ 1. Incentive plans always satisfy employee needs as well as the organization's needs.

1 _______ 2. The primary purpose of an incentive compensation plan is to ensure that employees have the opportunity to make some extra money under all circumstances

2 _______ 3. Straight piecework, one of the newest incentive plans is based on piecework.

2 _______ 4. Straight piecework employees receive a varying rate of pay for each unit produced.

2 _______ 5. One of the most significant weaknesses of piecework, as well as other incentive plans based on individual effort, is that it may not always be an effective motivator.

2 _______ 6. Piecework is appropriate where quality is more important than quantity.

2 _______ 7. Bonuses may be determined on the basis of cost reduction, quality improvement, or performance criteria established by the organization.

3 _______ 8. An advantage to receiving a single lump-sum merit payment is it can provide a clear link between pay and performance.

3 _______ 9. Research clearly shows that noncash incentive awards are most effective as motivators when the award is combined with a meaningful employee recognition program.

4 _______ 10. Some organizations have extended the salary range for professional positions to equal or nearly equal that for administrative positions.

4 _______ 11. An analysis of executive salaries shows that the largest portion of executive pay is received in short-term incentive rewards and bonuses.

4 _______ 12. Annual bonuses represent the main element of executive short-term incentives.

4 _______ 13. Most organizations pay their short-term incentive bonuses in the form of common stock to maintain their pay-for-performance strategy.

4 ________ 14. Balanced scorecards in terms of executive incentives are used to measure customer satisfaction, employee salary, and product or service leadership.

4 ________ 15. Perquisites are nonmonetary rewards given to executives.

5 ________ 16. The Scanlon Plan emphasizes participative management.

5 ________ 17. Under the Scanlon Plan, financial incentives based on increases in employee productivity are not offered to all employees, only executives.

5 ________ 18. The Scanlon Plan is an individual incentive plan.

5 ________ 19. Profit sharing plans are based on the organization's stock price.

5 ________ 20. Improshare output is measured by the number of finished products that a work team produces in a given period.

5 ________ 21. Improshare is a bonus plan based on dollar savings much like the Scanlon Plan.

5 ________ 22. Enterprise incentive plans reward employees on the basis of the success of the organization over an extended period of time—normally one year, but the period can be longer.

6 ________ 23. The purpose of profit sharing is to have employees commit to a specific area of the organization.

7 ________ 24. Employee stock ownership programs (ESOPs) are more likely to serve their intended purposes in privately held companies than in publicly held ones.

7 ________ 25. Although studies show that productivity improves when employee stock ownership plans are implemented, these gains are not guaranteed.

Matching

Match each term with the proper definition.

Terms

a. bonus
b. combined salary and commission plan
c. differential piece rate
d. employee stock ownership plans (ESOPs)
e. gainsharing plans
f. Improshare
k. salary plus bonus plan
l. Scanlon Plan
m. spot bonus
n. standard hour plan
o. straight commission plan
p. straight piecework

g. lump-sum merit program
h. merit guidelines
i. perquisites
j. profit sharing
q. straight salary plan
r. team incentive plan
s. variable pay

Definitions

_______ 1. gainsharing program under which bonuses are based on the overall productivity of the work team

_______ 2. compensation plan based on a percentage of sales

_______ 3. guidelines for awarding merit raises that are tied to performance objectives

_______ 4. incentive payment that is supplemental to the base wage

_______ 5. compensation plan that permits salespeople to be paid for performing various duties that are not reflected immediately in their sales volume

_______ 6. compensation plan that pays a salary plus bonus achieved by reaching targeted sales goals

_______ 7. stock plans in which an organization contributes shares of its stock to an established trust for the purpose of stock purchases by its employees

_______ 8. unplanned bonus given for employee effort unrelated to an established performance measure

_______ 9. compensation plan that includes a straight salary and a commission

_______ 10. special nonmonetary benefits often given to executives

_______ 11. programs under which both employees and the organization share the financial gains according to a predetermined formula that reflects improved productivity and profitability

_______ 12. compensation rate under which employees whose production exceeds the standard amount of output receive a higher rate for all of their work than the rate paid to those who do not exceed the standard amount

_______ 13. compensation plan in which all team members receive an incentive bonus payment when production or service standards are met or exceeded

_______14. incentive plan that sets rates based on the completion of a job in a predetermined standard time

_______15. program under which employees receive a year-end merit payment that is not added to their base pay

_______16. bonus incentive plan using employee and management committees to gain cost-reduction improvements

_______17. any procedure by which an employer pays or makes available to all regular employees, in addition to base pay, special current or deferred sums based on the profits of the enterprise

_______18. incentive plan under which employees receive a certain rate for each unit produced

_______19. tying pay to some measure of individual, group, or organizational performance

Internet Exercises

How can an employer reward loyal employees?
http://www.findarticles.com/p/articles/mi_m0DTI/is_4_32/ai_n6038412.

What is the relationship between profit-sharing and gainsharing plans?
http://www.findarticles.com/p/articles/mi_m0OGT/is_1_3/ai_n8690365.

How to Motivate Student Behavior

Motivation can be defined in terms of behavior. Students who are motivated exhibit a greater effort to perform a task than do those who are not motivated. Essentially, motivation is the willingness to do something, which is conditioned by the ability to satisfy some need for the student. For instance, the amount of effort a student puts into a class determines whether he or she will pass or fail. There are different theories that explain how student behavior is motivated. The expectancy theory proposes that motivation depends on how much a student wants something and how likely he or she thinks it is that the item will be received. If a student perceives that studying and researching will lead to a specific outcome, such as a good grade or a career goal, then he or she is motivated to perform the needed tasks.

Another theory of motivation for student behavior is Maslow's needs hierarchy theory. This theory states that there are five needs ranked in a hierarchical order from lowest to highest. These needs are physiological, safety, belonging, esteem, and self-actualization. A student has to satisfy the lower-level needs in order to move up through the hierarchy. A student who is motivated to excel in academics is attempting to satisfy the esteem and self-actualization needs. If the lower-level needs are not met, the student will experience difficulty in being motivated to perform well in his or her studies.

SOLUTIONS

Multiple Choice:

1. b
2. c
3. d
4. c
5. d
6. d
7. b
8. c
9. d
10. a
11. a
12. b
13. d
14. b
15. a
16. d
17. b
18. c
19. d
20. a
21. a
22. b
23. d
24. b
25. c
26. d
27. d
28. a
29. d
30. a

True/False:

1. False
2. False
3. False
4. False
5. True
6. False
7. True
8. True
9. True
10. True
11. False
12. True
13. False
14. False
15. True
16. True
17. False
18. False
19. False
20. True
21. False
22. True
23. False
24. False
25. True

Matching:

1. f
2. o
3. h
4. a
5. q
6. k
7. d
8. m
9. b
10. i
11. e
12. c
13. r
14. n
15. g
16. l
17. j
18. p
19. s

False Statements Made True

1. Incentive plans **sometimes fail to** satisfy employee needs as well as the organization's needs.
2. The primary **purposes** of an incentive compensation plan **are measurement and rewards**.
3. Straight piecework , one of the **oldest** incentive plans is based on piecework.
4. Straight piecework employees receive a **certain** rate of pay for each unit produced.
6. Piecework is **inappropriate** where quality is more important than quantity.
11. An analysis of executive salaries shows that the largest portion of executive pay is received in **long-term** incentive rewards and bonuses.
13. Most organizations pay their short-term incentive bonuses in the form of **annual profit plans, payments based on performance rating, and/or achievement of goals**.
14. Balanced scorecards in terms of executive incentives are used to measure customer satisfaction, the **ability to innovate**, and product or service leadership.
17. Under the Scanlon Plan, financial incentives based on increases in employee productivity **are offered to all hourly employees**.
18. The Scanlon Plan is a **group** incentive plan.
19. Profit sharing plans are based on an organization's **profits**.
21. Improshare is a bonus plan **not** based on dollar savings **but on productivity gains that result from reducing production time.**
23. The purpose of profit sharing is to **motivate a total commitment from employees rather than having them** commit to a specific area of the organization.
24. Employee stock ownership programs (ESOPs) are more likely to serve their intended purposes in **publicly** held companies than in **privately** held ones.

CHAPTER

11

EMPLOYEE BENEFITS

A growing portion of the compensation employees receive is not provided in their paycheck. Rather, it is paid in the form of benefits that employers increasingly must offer to compete in the labor market or to satisfy union demands or legal requirements. In order to emphasize that these benefits constitute a significant part of the compensation employees are paid, employers increasingly are using the term "total compensation." Different types of employee benefits entail different problems and costs.

LEARNING OBJECTIVES

After studying this chapter, you should be able to

1 Describe the characteristics of a sound benefits program.

2 Indicate management concerns about the costs of employee benefits, and discuss ways to control those costs.

3 Identify and explain the employee benefits required by law.

4 Discuss suggested ways to control the costs of health care programs.

5 Describe benefits that involve payment for time not worked.

6 Discuss the recent trends in retirement policies and programs.

7 Indicate the major factors involved in the management of pension plans.

8 Describe the types of work/life benefits that employers may provide.

CHAPTER SUMMARY RELATING TO LEARNING OBJECTIVES

1 Benefits are an established and integral part of the total compensation package. In order to have a sound benefits program, there are certain basic considerations. It is essential that a program be based on specific objectives that are compatible with organizational philosophy and policies as well as affordable. Through committees and surveys, a benefit package can be developed to meet employees' needs. Through the use of flexible benefit plans, employees are able to choose the benefits that are best suited for their individual needs. An important factor in how employees view the program is the full communication of benefits information through meetings, printed material, and annual personalized statements of benefits.

2 According to a 2007 study, the costs of employee benefits in that year averaged 42.7 percent of payroll or $21,527 per employee. Because many of the benefits represent a fixed cost, management must pay close attention in assuming more benefit expense. Increasingly, employers are requiring employees to pay part of the costs of certain benefits. Employers also shop for benefit services that are competitively priced.

3 Nearly a quarter of the benefits package that employers provide is legally required. These benefits include employer contributions to Social Security, unemployment insurance, workers' compensation insurance, and state disability insurance. Social Security taxes collected from employers and employees are used to pay three major types of benefits: (1) Retirement, (2) disability benefits, and (3) survivors' benefits.

4 The cost of healthcare programs has become the major concern in the area of employee benefits. Several approaches are used to contain healthcare costs, including reduction in coverage, increased coordination of benefits, increased deductibles or copayments, use of health maintenance and preferred provider organizations, various consumer-driven health plans, incentives for outpatient surgery and testing, and mandatory second opinions where surgery is indicated. Employee assistance programs and wellness programs may also contribute to cutting the costs of health care benefits.

5 Included in the category of benefits that involve payments for time not worked are vacations with pay, paid holidays, sick leave, and severance pay. The typical practice in the United States is to give ten days' vacation leave and ten holidays. In addition to vacation time, most employees, particularly in white-collar jobs, receive a set number of sick-leave days. A one-time payment of severance pay may be given to employees who are being terminated.

6 While there is no mandatory retirement age, many workers choose to retire before

age 65. Many employers provide incentives for early retirement in the form of increased pension benefits or cash bonuses. Some organizations provide preretirement programs that may include seminars, workshops, and informational materials. The National Council on Aging, the AARP and many other organizations are available to assist both employers and employees in preretirement activities.

7 Whether to offer a pension plan is the employer's prerogative. However, once a plan is established it is then subject to federal regulation under the Employee Retirement Income Security Act (ERISA) to ensure that benefits will be available when an employee retires. Two traditional pension plans are available – defined benefit and defined contribution. With a defined-benefit plan the amount an employee receives on retirement is based on years of service, average earnings, and age at time of retirement. Two of the most significant trends are the growth of 401(k) salary reduction plans and cash-balance pension plans. Pension funds may be administered through either a trusteed or an insurance plan. A concern today is the underfunding of pension plans and the ability of ERISA to meet its financial obligations.

8 The types of service benefits that employers typically provide include employee assistance programs, counseling services, educational assistance plans, child care, and elder care. Other benefits are food services, on-site health services, prepaid legal services, financial planning, housing and moving, transportation pooling, purchase assistance, credit unions, social and recreational services, and paycards.

REVIEW QUESTIONS

Multiple Choice

Choose the letter of the word or phrase that best completes each statement.

1 ______ 1. An indirect form of compensation intended to improve the quality of the work lives and the personal lives of employees is the
   a. incentive pay system.
   b. monetary wage.
   c. employee benefit plan.
   d. annual bonus plan.

1

_______ 2. The communication of employee benefits information improved significantly with passage of the
a. Equal Pay Act (EPA).
b. Fair Labor Standards Act.
c. Right to Privacy Act.
d. Employee Retirement Income Security Act (ERISA).

2

_______ 3. In managing an employee benefits program, management must consider the following, *except*
a. union demands.
b. benefits other employers are offering.
c. reengineering programs.
d. tax consequences.

3

_______ 4. Under the social security program, a fully insured person has earned
a. 40 credits.
b. 50 credits
c. 60 credits
d. 100 credits

3

_______ 5. How many workweeks of unpaid leave can an eligible employee take in a 12 month period under FMLA?
a. 10 weeks
b. 12 weeks
c. 14 weeks
d. 16 weeks

3

_______ 6. An act that provides an insurance plan designed to protect covered individuals against loss of earnings resulting from various causes is the
a. Equal Pay Act.
b. Social Security Act.
c. Civil Rights Act.
d. Employee Retirement Income Security Act.

3

_______ 7. Individual employees should not be required to bear the cost of their treatment or loss of income, nor should they be subjected to complicated, delaying, and expensive legal procedures under
a. workers' compensation insurance.
b. life insurance.
c. health insurance.
d. prescription optical insurance.

3 _______ 8. The benefits that receive the most attention from employers today because of high costs and employee concern are
a. overtime provisions.
b. prescription optical benefits.
c. child care benefits.
d. health care benefits.

4 _______ 9. Groups that offer routine medical services at a specific site for a fixed fee for each employee visit are called
a. prescription drug services.
b. rehabilitation services.
c. health maintenance organizations.
d. dental plans.

4 _______ 10. A medical insurance plan financed by employer contributions to an employee's individual health care spending account is a
a. supplemental pay benefit.
b. financial incentive.
c. consumer-driven health plan (CDHP).
d. job evaluation.

4 _______ 11. A plan in which enrolled individuals may make tax-free contributions to an account created primarily for the purpose of paying for qualified medical expenses is a(n)
a. medical savings account (MSA).
b. unemployment insurance program.
c. workers' compensation insurance plan.
d. Social Security insurance program.

4 _______ 12. The act that grants employees the right to switch their medical insurance between former and present employers is the
a. Occupational Safety and Health Act (OSHA).
b. Credit Reporting Act.
c. Employee Retirement Income and Security Act (ERISA).
d. Health Insurance Portability and Accountability Act (HIPAA).

4 _______ 13. With a diverse workforce, an increasing number of employers are willing to provide benefits to employees who establish
a. domestic partnership.
b. health maintenance organizations (HMOs).
c. human resources plans.
d. employee vesting.

4

_______ 14. The following are standards that enable an employee to qualify under a domestic partnership in an organization, *except*

a. minimum age requirement.
b. specification of financial independence.
c. requirement that the couple live together.
d. requirement that the relationship be a permanent one.

5

_______ 15. The category of benefits that includes paid vacations, bonuses given in lieu of paid vacations, payments for holidays not worked, paid sick leave, military and jury duty, and payments for absence due to a death in the family or other personal reasons is called

a. unemployment insurance.
b. payment for time not worked.
c. Social Security insurance.
d. payment for time worked.

5

_______ 16. A one-time payment, usually dependent on an individual's years of service, that is given to employees who are being terminated is

a. unemployment insurance.
b. supplemental unemployment benefits (SUBs).
c. vacation pay.
d. severance pay.

5

_______ 17. Insurance designed to pay for nursing home and other medical costs during old age is known as

a. long-term care insurance.
b. prescription optical insurance.
c. prescription drug insurance.
d. workers' compensation insurance.

6

_______ 18. The baby boom generation is a demographic group born between

a. 1946 and 1964
b. 1964 and 1984.
c. 1984 and 2004
d. 2004 and today.

6

_______ 19. An early-retirement incentive in the form of increased pension benefits for several years or a cash bonus is referred to as the

a. employer buy-out.
b. silver handshake.
c. labor contract.
d. employee sick bank.

7

_______ 20. The type of pension plan in which the amount an employee is to receive upon retirement is specifically set forth is the
a. voluntary fringe plan.
b. noncontributory holiday plan.
c. involuntary benefit plan.
d. defined-benefit plan.

7

_______ 21. The type of pension plan in which contributions are jointly made by employers and employees is a/an
a. voluntary fringe plan.
b. noncontributory holiday plan.
c. involuntary benefit plan.
d. contributory plan

7

_______ 22. A tax-deferred plan that allows employees to save through payroll deductions and to have their contributions matched by the employer is known as
a. supplemental unemployment benefits (SUBs).
b. unemployment insurance.
c. a 401(k) savings plan.
d. Social Security insurance.

7

_______ 23. A guarantee of accrued benefits to participants at retirement age, regardless of their employment status at the time, is known as
a. portability.
b. vestibule training.
c. piece rate.
d. vesting.

7

_______ 24. Private pension plans are subject to federal regulation under the
a. National Labor Relations Act.
b. Employee Retirement Income Security Act (ERISA).
c. National Industry Recovery Act.
d. Truth and Lending Law.

8

_______ 25. To help workers cope with a wide variety of problems that interfere with job performance, organizations have developed
a. employee assistance programs.
b. 401(k) plans.
c. severance pay packages.
d. contributory plans.

8

_______ 26. A portion of a worker's pay before taxes is set aside for a dependent child with a
a. health insurance plan.
b. pension program.
c. dependent-care spending account.
d. counseling service.

8

_______ 27. The benefit provided to an older relative by an employee who remains actively at work is called
a. elder care.
b. dental insurance.
c. life insurance.
d. health insurance.

8

_______ 28. To reduce the negative effects of caregiving on productivity, organizations may offer
a. elder care seminars.
b. elder care support groups.
c. leaves of absence for elder care.
d. all of the above.

8

_______ 29. Financial planning programs cover all of the following, *except*
a. retirement planning.
b. tax planning and management.
c. estate planning.
d. food services.

8

_______ 30. Which of the following programs are seen as a hedge against talent drain and also as encouraging employee retention?
a. retirement planning.
b. tax planning and management.
c. estate planning.
d. educational assistance

True/False

Identify the following statements as True or False.

1 ______ 1. Like any other component of the human resources program, an employee benefits program should be based on specific objectives.

1 ______ 2. Before a new benefit is introduced, the need for it should first be determined through a consultation with customers.

1 ______ 3. To accommodate the individual needs of employees, there is a trend toward flexible benefits plans, also known as cafeteria plans.

2 ______ 4. Since many benefits represent a variable rather than a fixed cost, management must decide whether or not it can afford this cost under less favorable economic conditions.

2 ______ 5. Organizations that offer benefits to domestic partners are simply extending current benefits, normally full medical and dental plans, to employees.

2 ______ 6. Legally required employee benefits constitute nearly a quarter of the benefits package that employers provide.

3 ______ 7. To be eligible for old-age and survivors' insurance as well as for disability and unemployment insurance under the Social Security Act, an individual need not be engaged in employment covered by the act.

3 ______ 8. Workers' compensation laws typically provide that employees will be paid a disability benefit based on work performance.

3 ______ 9. A covered employer must grant an eligible employee up to a total of two workweeks of unpaid leave in a two-month period under the Family and Medical Leave Act.

4 ______ 10. The approaches used to contain the costs of health care benefits include reductions in coverage, increased deductibles or co-payments, and increased coordination of benefits.

4 ______ 11. The preferred provider organization (PPO) is a group of physicians who establish an organization through lower service charges or agreed-upon utilization controls.

4 ______ 12. A supplemental pay benefit allows employees to select a doctor of their choice from a list of physicians.

5 ______ 13. A supplemental unemployment benefits plan enables an employee who is working to draw weekly benefits, in addition to state unemployment compensation, from the employer.

5 _______ 14. One of the oldest and most popular employee benefits is group term life insurance, which provides death benefits to beneficiaries and may also provide accidental death and dismemberment benefits.

6 _______ 15. To encourage layoffs, particularly of more recently hired members of protected classes, and to reduce salary and benefit costs, employers often encourage early retirement.

6 _______ 16. Due to the vesting requirements negotiated into most union contracts and more recently required by law, pensions are now based on a reward philosophy.

7 _______ 17. In a contributory plan, contributions are made solely by the employer.

7 _______ 18. When pension plans are classified by the amount of pension benefits to be paid, there are two basic types: the defined-benefit plan and the defined-contribution plan.

7 _______ 19. Unlike traditional defined-benefit pension plans, which guarantee payments based on years of service, the 401(k) plans guarantee nothing.

7 _______ 20. An employer can revoke vested pension benefits that have been earned by an employee.

7 _______ 21. Managers and supervisors should remember that antidiscrimination laws apply to the administration of benefit programs.

8 _______ 22. The increased employment of women with dependent children has created an unprecedented demand for childcare arrangements.

8 _______ 23. Demand for elder care programs will decrease dramatically as baby boomers move into their fifties and find themselves managing organizations.

8 _______ 24. Although the employer may provide office space and a payroll deduction service, employee services such as the use of credit unions are operated by the employees under federal and state legislation and supervision.

8 _______ 25. Many organizations do not offer some type of sports program in which personnel may participate on a voluntary basis.

Matching

Match each term with the proper definition.

Terms

a. consumer driven health plan
b. contributory plan
c. defined-benefit plan
d. defined-contribution plan
e. elder care
f. employee assistance programs (EAPs)
g. flexible benefits plans (cafeteria plans)
h. health maintenance organizations (HMOs)
i. noncontributory plan
j. preferred provider organization (PPO)
k. silver handshake
l. supplemental unemployment benefits (SUBs)
m. vesting
n. workers' compensation insurance

Definitions

_______ 1. benefit plans that enable individual employees to choose the benefits that are best suited to their particular needs

_______ 2. a guarantee of accrued benefits to participants at retirement age, regardless of their employment status at that time

_______ 3. organizations of physicians and health care professionals that provide a wide range of services to subscribers and dependents on a prepaid basis

_______ 4. care provided to an elderly relative by an employee who remains actively at work

_______ 5. federal- or state-mandated insurance provided to workers to defray the loss of income and cost of treatment due to work-related injuries or illness

_______ 6. a pension plan in which contributions are made jointly by employees and employers

_______ 7. a pension plan in which contributions are made solely by the employer

_______ 8. services provided by employers to help workers cope with a wide variety of problems that interfere with the way they perform their jobs

_______ 9. a plan that enables an employee who is laid off to draw weekly benefits, in addition to state unemployment compensation, from the employer that are paid from a fund created for this purpose

_______ 10. a pension plan in which the amount an employee is to receive upon retirement is specifically set forth

_______ 11. an early-retirement incentive in the form of increased pension benefits for several years or a cash bonus

_______ 12. a pension plan that establishes the basis on which an employer will contribute to the pension fund

_______ 13. a group of physicians who establish an organization that guarantees lower health care costs to the employer

_______ 14. a medical insurance plan financed by employer contributions to an employee's individual health care spending account

Internet Exercise

What are the benefits of cafeteria plans?
http://www.entrepreneur.com/humanresources/compensationandbenefits/article79978.html

How to Recognize the Importance of Fringe Benefits

Employee benefits generally comprise various rewards, incentives, and other rights of value that an organization provides to its employees beyond their wages, salaries, and other forms of direct financial compensation. A benefits program should be more than a laundry list of specific entitlements. It should be a well-developed package of benefits and benefit options that best fulfill the needs of employees and the organization.

There are several types of fringe benefits offered by employers. Laws mandate that all employees must have certain benefits such as Social Security, unemployment insurance, and worker's compensation. Other benefits include health and dental plans, private pension plans, and paid time off in the form of vacation time, holiday pay, sick leave, and personal time. Employers have also included in their benefits package wellness programs, child care, elder care, and employee assistance programs.

Probably the most important option is health care coverage. While law does not mandate this benefit, it has become standard. With the increasing cost of health care and the rise of managed care, this benefit has been a major concern for employees. The ideal plan is one in which the employer gives the employee options and pays for a significant portion of the costs.

A popular type of benefit package is a cafeteria-style plan. This often is the best alternative because it allows employees to choose the benefits they really want. Employees are given a list of benefits and costs, and they can choose any combination that best serves their needs. This has become increasingly important with the rise of two-income families. One spouse may have a better health plan with an employer. This plan would allow the other spouse to elect another benefit option and reduce the costs. It also provides flexibility in the benefit selection process. Employees should analyze the benefit options offered by potential employers, and weigh the employment decision accordingly.

SOLUTIONS

Multiple Choice:

1. c
2. d
3. c
4. a
5. b
6. b
7. a
8. d
9. c
10. c
11. a
12. d
13. a
14. b
15. b
16. d
17. a
18. a
19. b
20. d
21. d

True/False:

1. True
2. False
3. True
4. False
5. True
6. True
7. False
8. False
9. False
10. True
11. True
12. False
13. False
14. True
15. False
16. False
17. False
18. True
19. True
20. False
21. True

Matching:

1. g
2. m
3. h
4. e
5. n
6. b
7. i
8. f
9. l
10. c
11. k
12. d
13. j
14. a

22. c
23. d
24. b
25. a
26. c
27. a
28. d
29. d
30. d

22 True
23. False
24. True
25. False

False Statements Made True

2. Before a new benefit is introduced, the need for it should first be determined through a consultation with **employees**.
4. Since many benefits represent a **fixed** rather than a **variable** cost, management must decide whether or not it can afford this cost under less favorable economic conditions.
7. To be eligible for old-age and survivors' insurance as well as for disability and unemployment insurance under the Social Security Act, an individual **must** be engaged in employment covered by the act.
8. Workers' compensation laws typically provide that employees will be paid a disability benefit based on **a percentage of their wages**.
9. A covered employer must grant an eligible employee up to a total of **twelve** workweeks of unpaid leave in a **twelve**-month period under the Family and Medical Leave Act.
12. A **preferred provider organization** allows employees to select a doctor of their choice from a list of physicians.
13. A supplemental unemployment benefits plan enables an employee who is **laid off** to draw weekly benefits, in addition to state unemployment compensation, from the employer.
15. To **avoid** layoffs, particularly of more recently hired members of protected classes, and to reduce salary and benefit costs, employers often encourage early retirement.
16. Due to the vesting requirements negotiated into most union contracts and more recently required by law, pensions are now based on **an earnings** philosophy.
17. In a **noncontributory** plan, contributions are made solely by the employer.
20. An employer **cannot** revoke vested pension benefits that have been earned by an employee.
23. Demand for elder care programs will **increase** dramatically as baby boomers move into their fifties and find themselves managing organizations.
25. Many organizations **do offer** some type of sports program in which personnel may participate on a voluntary basis.

CHAPTER

12

PROMOTING SAFETY AND HEALTH

Safety and health programs have continued to receive employer attention since the passage of the Occupational Safety and Health Act (OSHA). For several reasons discussed in the text, employers have intensified their efforts to create safe work environments. Similarly, they have developed programs to reduce health hazards on the job. Many employers have instituted programs for building better health and for providing assistance to employees. They have developed stress-management programs to teach employees how to minimize the negative effects of job-related stress.

LEARNING OBJECTIVES

After studying this chapter, you should be able to

1 Summarize the general provisions of the Occupational Safety and Health Act (OSHA).

2 Describe what management can do to create a safe work environment.

3 Identify the measures that should be taken to control and eliminate health hazards.

4 Describe the organizational services and programs for building better health.

5 Explain the role of employee assistance programs in HRM.

6 Indicate methods for coping with stress.

CHAPTER SUMMARY RELATING TO LEARNING OBJECTIVES

1 The Occupational Safety and Health Act was designed to assure, so far as possible, safe and healthful working conditions for every working person. In general, the act extends to all employers and employees. OSHA administration involves setting standards, ensures employer and employee compliance, and provides safety and health consultation and training where needed. Both employers and employees have certain responsibilities and rights under OSHA. Employers not only are required to provide a hazard-free work environment but also must keep employees informed about the OSHA requirements and must require their employees to use protective equipment when necessary. Under the "right to know" regulation, employers are required to keep employees informed of hazardous substances and instruct them in avoiding the dangers presented. Employees, in turn, are required to comply with the OSHA standards, to report hazardous conditions, and to follow all employer safety and health regulations.

2 In order to provide safe working conditions for their employees, employers typically establish a formal program that, in a large percentage of organizations, is under the direction of the HR manager. The program may have many facets, including providing safety knowledge and motivating employees to use it, making employees aware of the need for safety, and rewarding them for safe behavior. Such incentives as praise, public recognition, and awards are used to involve employees in the safety program. Maintenance of required records from accident investigations provides a basis for information that can be used to create a safer work environment.

3 Job conditions that are dangerous to the health of employees are now receiving much greater attention than in the past. There is special concern for toxic chemicals that proliferate at a rapid rate and may lurk in the body for years without outward symptoms. Health hazards other than those found in manufacturing operations, such as video display terminals, and cumulative trauma disorders present special problems that must be addressed. Today tobacco smoke is rarely tolerated in the work environment. While there is no evidence that AIDS can be spread through casual contact in the workplace, employers have found that it is important to educate managers and employees about AIDS and to assist those who have it.

4 Along with providing safer and healthier work environments, many employers establish programs that encourage employees to improve their health habits. Some of the larger employers have opened primary care clinics for employees and their dependents to provide better health care service and to reduce costs. Wellness programs that emphasize exercise, nutrition, weight control, and avoidance of harmful substances serve employees at all organizational levels.

5 Virtually all of the larger organizations and many smaller ones have found that an employee assistance program is beneficial to all concerned. While emotional problems, personal crises, alcoholism, and drug abuse are often viewed as personal matters, it is apparent that they affect behavior at work and interfere with job performance. An employee assistance program typically provides professional assistance by in-house counselors or outside professionals where needed.

6 An important dimension to health and safety is stress that comes from physical activity and mental or emotional activity. While stress is an integral part of being alive, when it turns into distress it becomes harmful. We have seen that many sources of stress are job related. In recognizing the need for reducing stress, employers can develop stress-management programs to help employees learn techniques for coping with stress. In addition, organizations need to redesign and enrich jobs, clarify the employee's work role, correct physical factors in the environment, and take any other actions that will help reduce stress on the job.

Done 10/19/11

REVIEW QUESTIONS

-7

Multiple Choice

Choose the letter of the word or phrase that best completes each statement.

1 __c__ 1. The act that has been very effective in reducing the number of injuries resulting in lost work time, the incident rate of specific injuries, and the number of job-related deaths is the
   a. Equal Pay Act.
   b. Age Discrimination and Employment Act.
   c. Occupational Safety and Health Act (OSHA).
   d. Pregnancy Leave Act.

1 __b__ 2. One of the responsibilities of the Occupational Safety and Health Administration is to develop and enforce
   a. mandatory pregnancy sick days.
   b. mandatory job safety and health standards.
   c. equal pay for equal work.
   d. nondiscriminatory applications pertaining to age requirements.

1 A

3. The Occupational Safety and Health Administration can cite an employer for any of the following types of violations, *except*
   a. discipline procedure violations.
   b. other-than-serious violations.
   c. serious violations.
   d. willful violations.

1 D

4. The Occupational Safety and Health Administration may propose penalties of up to $70,000 for each act of which type of violation?
   a. discipline procedure violations.
   b. other-than-serious violations.
   c. serious violations.
   d. willful violations.

1 D B

5. The government agency that provides a free on-site safety consultation service is the
   a. Federal Trail Commission.
   b. Occupational Safety and Health Administration.
   c. Food and Drug Administration.
   d. National Labor Relations Board.

1 D

6. Which cooperative program provides recognition to employers who demonstrate exemplary achievement in workplace health and safety?
   a. voluntary retirement programs.
   b. employer associations.
   c. affirmative action programs.
   d. safety and health achievement recognition program.

1 B

7. The definition of toxic and hazardous substances, the duties of employers and manufacturers to provide health-risk information to employees, trade-secret protection, and enforcement provisions are statutes addressed under
   a. pregnancy leave.
   b. employee right-to-know laws.
   c. business necessity actions.
   d. bona fide occupational qualifications.

2 ______ 8. The most important purpose of a safety awareness program is to promote awareness of safety considerations among the following people in an organization, *except*

a. customers.
b. managers.
c. supervisors.
d. subordinates.

2 ______ 9. Many organizations cover first aid, defensive driving, accident prevention techniques, handling of hazardous materials, and emergency procedures in their

a. affirmative action policy.
b. safety and health training.
c. business ethics code.
d. mission statement.

2 ______ 10. Computer training techniques to enhance safety awareness would include the following, *except*

a. e-tools.
b. interactive CD-ROMs.
c. Local Area Networks.
d. PowerPoint presentations.

2 ______ 11. Specific rules and regulations concerning safety are communicated through

a. bulletin board notices.
b. employee handbooks.
c. signs attached to equipment.
d. all of the above.

2 ______ 12. A recordable case is any injury or illness that results in any of the following, *except*

a. death.
b. days away from work.
c. restricted work or transfer to another job.
d. vacation.

3 ______ 13. The U.S. Supreme in the *Johnson Controls (1991)* case ruled that employers may not

a. bar women from certain jobs due to risk of sexual harassment.
b. bar women of childbearing age from certain jobs because of potential risk to their fetuses.

c. bar women from bringing their children to work on Sundays.
d. reduce indoor air quality on holidays.

3 C 14. Mini-breaks that involve exercises, properly designed workstations, the changing of positions, and improvement in tool design are ways an organization can prevent
a. sexual harassment.
b. chemical hazards.
c. cumulative trauma disorders.
d. indoor air quality.

3 B 15. The "deadly virus" of crime in American work environments is
a. second-hand smoke.
b. workplace violence.
c. job burnout.
d. video display terminals hazards.

3 D 16. To minimize the consequences of terrorism, organizations are implementing
a. emergency evacuation procedures.
b. background checks.
c. blast resistant glass.
d. all of the above.

3 A 17. Organizations that have employees who conduct initial risk assessment surveys, develop action plans to respond to violent situations, and perform crisis intervention during violent or potentially violent encounters have established
a. crisis management teams.
b. wellness programs.
c. employee right-to-know laws.
d. citation committees.

3 D 18. Along with improving working conditions that are hazardous to employee health, many employers provide health services and have programs that encourage employees to improve their
a. alarm reactions.
b. resistance to job burnout.
c. financial status.
d. health habits.

4 ___C___ 19. Currently, one of the more critical health and wellness issues facing employers—as well as Americans in general—is
a. smoking.
b. high blood pressure.
c. overweight and obesity.
d. high cholesterol.

4 ___D___ 20. According to Center for Disease Control, what percent of Americans are overweight?
a. 34%
b. 44%
c. 54%
d. 64%

5 ___C___ 21. A program referring employees in need of assistance to in-house counselors or outside professionals is a(n)
a. employee right-to-know program.
b. alarm reaction program.
c. employee assistance program.
d. voluntary protection program (VPP).

5 ___B___ 22. When managers note that individual productivity is lowered, that morale problems exist, and that absenteeism and substance abuse are increasing, they are identifying the signs of
a. employee satisfaction.
b. employee depression.
c. union busting.
d. external environmental controls.

5 ___A___ 23. Today one of the major employment issues affecting individuals is
a. drug abuse.
b. recycling of products.
c. global warming.
d. acid rain.

5 ___B D___ 24. Awakening the person to the reality of his or her situation is the first step in helping the
a. individual through cultural shock.
b. wellness committee.
c. union organizing drive.
d. alcoholic.

5 ______ 25. Which act requires federal contractors and recipients of federal grants to take specific steps to ensure a drug-free work environment?
a. The Drug-Free Workplace Act
b. Americans with Disabilities Act
c. Equal Pay Act
d. Fair Labor Standards Act .

6 ______ 26. Physical activity and mental or emotional activity are two basic sources of
a. job performance.
b. employee turnover.
c. chronic absenteeism.
d. stress.

6 ______ 27. Positive stress that accompanies achievement and exhilaration is
a. distress.
b. alarm reaction.
c. eustress.
d. job enrichment.

6 ______ 28. Harmful stress characterized by a loss of feelings of security and adequacy is called
a. distress.
b. alarm reaction.
c. eustress.
d. job enrichment.

6 ______ 29. High demand, high effort, low control, and low reward are identified as the primary factors in
a. marital success.
b. employee orientation.
c. employee stress.
d. employee training.

6 ______ 30. The most severe stage of distress, manifesting itself in depression, frustration, and loss of productivity, is
a. burnout.
b. anxiety.
c. nervousness.
d. fatigue.

True/False

Identify the following statements as True or False.

1 _____ 1. Improved productivity and wages and the lack of medical expenses coupled with decreased disabilities in the workplace led to the passage of the Occupational Safety and Health Act in 1970.

1 _____ 2. The *Federal Register* is the principal source of information on proposed, adopted, amended, and deleted Occupational Safety and Health Act standards.

1 _____ 3. Typically, the Occupational Safety and Health Act inspectors will arrive at a work site unannounced and ask for a meeting with a representative of the employer.

1 _____ 4. The Occupational Safety and Health Act citations may be issued immediately following inspections or later by mail.

1 _____ 5. Employees are not required to comply with all applicable Occupational Safety and Health Act standards, to report hazardous conditions, and to follow all employer safety and health rules and regulations, including those prescribing the use of protective equipment.

1 _____ 6. The complaint most registered against the Occupational Safety and Health Administration is the even enforcement efforts by the agency from one political administration to the next.

2 _____ 7. To achieve safe working conditions, the majority of employers have an informal safety program.

2 _____ 8. One of a supervisor's major responsibilities is to communicate to employees the need to work safely.

2 _____ 9. Human resources professionals and safety directors do not encourage employee involvement when designing and implementing safety programs.

2 _____ 10. Penalties for violating safety rules are usually stated in the employee handbook.

2 _____ 11. The supervisor and a member of the safety committee do not need to investigate every accident.

2 _____ 12. The Occupational Safety and Health Act requirements mandate that employers with 11 or more employees maintain records of occupational injuries and illnesses.

2 ______ 13. An injury or illness is a recordable case if it results in death, days away from work, restricted work, transfer to another job, or medical treatment beyond first aid.

3 ______ 14. The Occupational Safety and Health Act is clearly designed to protect the health, as well as the safety, of employees.

3 ______ 15. Hazardous chemical containers do not have to be labeled with the identity of the contents but must state any appropriate hazard warnings.

3 ______ 16. When cumulative trauma disorders result from work activities, these injuries have been held by courts to be compensable injuries entailing workers' compensation payments.

3 ______ 17. It is recognized that better health not only benefits the individual but also pays off for the organization in reduced absenteeism, increased efficiency, better morale, and other savings.

5 ______ 18. Emotional problems, personal crises, alcoholism, and drug abuse are considered to be personal matters that are never organizational problems.

5 ______ 19. The most prevalent problems among employees are personal crises involving marital, family, financial, or legal matters.

5 ______ 20. The National Institute of Mental Health estimates that nearly 17 million Americans suffer from some form of physical impairment every year.

5 ______ 21. In confronting the problem, employers must recognize that alcoholism is a disease that follows a rather unpredictable course.

5 ______ 22. Alcoholism is regarded as a disease and is always treated as a physical impairment of the employee.

6 ______ 23. Stress becomes distress when a person begins to sense a loss of feelings of security and adequacy.

6 ______ 24. Career burnout, a severe stage of distress, generally occurs when a person begins questioning company values.

6 ______ 25. Individual employees in good physical health are immune to stressors in the work environment.

Matching

Match each term with the proper definition.

13

Terms

a. incidence rate
b. burnout
c. cumulative trauma disorders
d. depression
e. distress
f. right-to-know laws
g. eustress
h. Material Safety Data Sheets (MSDSs)
i. recordable case
j. stress

Definitions

C 1. injuries involving tendons of the fingers, hands, and arms that become inflamed from repeated stresses and strains

D 2. negative emotional state marked by feelings of low spirits, gloominess, sadness, and loss of pleasure in ordinary activities

B (E) X 3. harmful stress characterized by a loss of feelings of security and adequacy

I (A) X 4. The number of injuries and illnesses per 100 full-time employees during a given year.

H 5. documents that contain vital information about hazardous substances

G 6. positive stress that accompanies achievement and exhilaration

J 7. any adjustive demand caused by physical, mental, or emotional factors that requires coping behavior

F 8. laws that require employers to advise employees of job hazards

A (B) X 9. most severe stage of distress, manifesting itself in depression, frustration, and loss of productivity

I 10. any occupational death, illness, or injury to be recorded in the Occupational Safety and Health Act log

Internet Exercises

What are the job factors that contribute to employee burnout?
http://stress.about.com/od/burnout/a/job_burnout.htm

What actions would you recommended to address workplace tragedy?
http://humanresources.about.com/od/healthsafetyandwellness/a/tragedy_work.htm

How to Inquire about a Safe and Healthy Work Environment

You are encouraged to inquire about a safe and healthy work environment with prospective employers. Safety is an important concern to everyone, and questions should be generated based on the philosophy of management and the firm's commitment to
safety. Ask questions related to safety issues, such as the following: What are the major causes of accidents in the workplace? Does the Occupational Safety and Health Act regulate this work environment? Does the employer presently have a safety committee? What is its role and function? Is it a recommending body or does it have functional authority? Does the employer have a logbook to record accidents?

Health-related factors are important concerns for employees and should be addressed. Health hazards are those characteristics of the work environment that more slowly and systematically result in damage to the employee's health. Thus, health hazards impair working conditions and can result in decreased productivity and downtime. There are Occupational Safety and Health Act regulations pertaining to health requirements. You should address health-related issues, such as exposure to hazardous chemicals or toxic substances. Employers must disclose information to employees concerning any hazard that may pose an injury to their health. A smoking policy is becoming an important issue due to the increased hazard of second-hand smoke. For instance, smoking is prohibited in most state and federal offices. There are procedures and rules that may apply, and you are encouraged to become familiar with these regulations.

SOLUTIONS

Multiple Choice:	True/False:	Matching:
1. c	1. False	1. c
2. b	2. True	2. d
3. a	3. True	3. e
4. d	4. True	4. a
5. b	5. False	5. h
6. d	6. False	6. g
7. b	7. False	7. j
8. a	8. True	8. f
9. b	9. False	9. b
10. c	10. True	10. i
11. d	11. False	
12. d	12. True	
13. b	13. True	
14. c	14. True	
15. b	15. False	
16. d	16. True	
17. a	17. True	
18. d	18. False	
19. c	19. True	
20. d	20. False	
21. c	21. False	
22. b	22. False	
23. a	23. True	
24. d	24. False	
25. a	25. False	
26. d		
27. c		
28. a		
29. c		
30. a		

False Statements Made True

1. **Lost** productivity and wages and **increasing** medical expenses coupled with **increased** disabilities in the workplace led to the passage of the Occupational Safety and Health Act in 1970.
5. Employees **are** required to comply with all applicable Occupational Safety and Health Act standards, to report hazardous conditions, and to follow all employer

safety and health rules and regulations, including those prescribing the use of protective equipment.

6. The complaint most registered against the Occupational Safety and Health Administration is the **uneven** enforcement efforts by the agency from one political administration to the next.
7. To achieve safe working conditions, the majority of employers have **a formal** safety program.
9. Human resources professionals and safety directors **advocate** employee involvement when designing and implementing safety programs.
11. The supervisor and a member of the safety committee **need** to investigate every accident.
15. Hazardous chemical containers **must** be labeled with the identity of the contents **and** must state any appropriate hazard warnings.
18. Emotional problems, personal crises, alcoholism, and drug abuse are considered to be personal matters that **become** organizational problems.
20. The National Institute of Mental Health estimates that nearly 17 million Americans suffer from **depression** every year.
21. In confronting the problem, employers must recognize that alcoholism is a disease that follows a rather **predictable** course.
22. Alcoholism is regarded as a disease **similar to a mental impairment** of the employee.
24. Career burnout, a severe stage of distress, generally occurs when a person begins questioning **his or her own personal** values.
25. Individuals in good physical health are **better able to cope with** stressors in the work environment.

PART FIVE

Enhancing Employee-Management Relations

CHAPTER 13

EMPLOYEE RIGHTS AND DISCIPLINE

The rights of employees to protect their jobs while obtaining fair and just treatment from employers received much attention during the 1990s. On the other side of the balance are the employer's responsibilities to provide a safe and efficient workplace for employees while expecting productivity and a positive attitude from all jobholders. Issues such as drug testing, smoking on the job, access to one's personnel file, notice of plant closing, and unfair discharge are therefore topics of interest to all organizational members.

When employees exhibit unsatisfactory behavior or performance, it may be necessary for an employer to take disciplinary action against them. If the employee is represented by a union, the disciplinary action is likely to be appealed through the grievance procedure provided for in the labor agreement. In a nonunion organization, the aggrieved employee may use an alternative dispute-resolution procedure established specifically by the employer. In either the union or nonunion setting, management may ultimately have to defend its position to a specified individual or group who will decide on the reasonableness of the action taken. To defend themselves successfully, as well as to simply impose fair and objective disciplinary procedures, supervisors and managers need to understand the principles of effective discipline.

Organizational ethics extends beyond the legal requirements of managing employees in human resources management. Managers must comply with governmental regulations to promote an environment free from litigation. However, beyond what is required by law are the matters of organizational ethics and the ethical or unethical behavior engaged in by managers.

LEARNING OBJECTIVES

After studying this chapter, you should be able to

1. Explain the concepts of employee rights and employer responsibilities.

2. Explain the concepts of employment at will, wrongful discharge, implied contract, and constructive discharge.

3. Identify and explain the privacy rights of employees.

4 Explain the process of establishing disciplinary policies, including the proper implementation of organizational rules.

5 Discuss the meaning of discipline and how to investigate a disciplinary problem.

6 Differentiate between the two approaches to disciplinary action.

7 Identify the different types of alternative dispute resolution procedures.

8 Discuss the role of ethics in the management of human resources.

CHAPTER SUMMARY RELATING TO LEARNING OBJECTIVES

1 Employees may claim that they have legal rights guaranteeing them fair and equitable treatment while on the job. Employee rights issues frequently involve employer searches, drug testing, and monitoring of an employee's personal conversation. Employers, however, have the responsibility to provide a safe and secure workplace free from harmful employee acts. When the perceived rights of employees differ with the reasonable responsibilities of management, conflict can result.

2 Both employees and employers have rights and expectations in the employment relationship. The employment-at-will doctrine regards the rights of employees and employers to terminate the employment relationship, the implied-contract concept is an exception to the employment-at-will doctrine. Under this concept, an employer's oral or written statements may form a contractual obligation that can preclude the automatic termination of employees. Constructive discharge occurs when an employee voluntarily terminates employment but subsequently alleges he or she was forced to quit because of intolerable working conditions imposed by the employer. Employees may claim they are being retaliated against when employers punish them for exercising their rights under law or for receiving favorable Equal Employment Opportunity Commission or court awards.

3 Once employed, employees expect certain privacy rights regarding freedom from unwarranted intrusion into their personal affairs. These rights extend over such issues as substance abuse and drug testing; searches and monitoring; off-duty privacy rights, email, internet, and voice mail privacy, and genetic testing.

4 The human resources department, in combination with other managers, should establish disciplinary policies. This will help achieve both acceptance of the policy and its consistent application. To reduce the need for discipline, organizational rules and procedures should be widely known, reviewed on a regular basis, and written, and explained to employees. The rules must relate to the safe and efficient operation of the organization. When managers overlook the enforcement of rules, they must reemphasize the rule and its enforcement before disciplining an employee.

5 The term "discipline" has three meanings—punishment, orderly behavior, and the training of employee conduct. When used with employees, discipline should serve to correct undesirable employee behavior, creating within the employee a desire for self-control. This third definition of discipline can be achieved only when managers conduct a complete and unbiased investigation of employee misconduct. Investigation of employee misconduct begins with the proper documentation of wrongdoing. When managers are investigating employee problems they need to know specifically the infraction of the employee, whether the employee knew of the rule violated, and any extenuating circumstances that might justify the employee's conduct. When employees are to receive discipline, the rule must be uniformly enforced and the past work record of the employee must be considered.

6 The two approaches to discipline are progressive discipline and positive discipline. Progressive discipline follows a series of steps based on increasing the degrees of corrective action. The corrective action applied should match the severity of the employee misconduct. Positive discipline, based upon reminders, is a cooperative discipline approach in which employees accept responsibility for the desired employee improvement. The focus is on coping with the unsatisfactory performance and dissatisfactions of employees before the problems become major.

7 Alternative dispute resolution procedures present ways by which employees exercise their due process rights. The most common forms of alternative dispute-resolutions (ADRs) are step-review systems, peer-review systems, the open-door system, the ombudsman system, mediation, and arbitration.

8 Ethics in HRM management extends beyond the legal requirements of managing employees. Managers engage in ethical behavior when employees are treated in an objective and fair way and when an employee's personal and work-related rights are respected and valued.

REVIEW QUESTIONS

Multiple Choice

Choose the letter of the word or phrase that best completes each statement.

1

_______ 1. The guarantee of fair treatment that employees expect in protection of their employment status is
a. employee rights.
b. equal pay for equal work.
c. fair employment.
d. performance appraisal.

1

_______ 2. The failure to provide a reasonable amount of care where such failure results in injury to another person is
a. punishment.
b. suspension.
c. negligence.
d. severance pay.

2

_______ 3. When an employee agrees to work for an employer for an unspecified period, the resulting relationship is called
a. alternative dispute resolution.
b. business ethics.
c. employment-at-will.
d. negligence.

2

_______ 4. In *Adair v. United States* the Supreme Court upheld
a. alternative dispute resolution programs.
b. the need for ethical behavior in firms.
c. employment-at-will doctrine.
d. negligence doctrine.

2

_______ 5. Which agency administers the whistle-blowing provisions in 15 federal statutes?
a. EEOC
b. OSHA
c. NLRB
d. FCC

2 _______ 6. Agreements that prohibit ex-employees from soliciting clients or customers of former employers for a specified period of time are called
a. non-compete agreements.
b. intellectual property agreement.
c. non-piracy agreements.
d. employment-at-will agreements.

2 _______ 7. Oral or written statements made during the preemployment process or subsequent to hiring are
a. employment-at-will contracts.
b. employee rights.
c. business ethics.
d. implied contractual rights.

2 _______ 8. An employee's voluntary termination of his or her employment because of harsh, unreasonable employment conditions placed upon the individual by the employer is called
a. employee assistance.
b. constructive discharge.
c. human resources planning.
d. job evaluation.

2 _______ 9. WARN Act requires organizations with more than 100 employees to give employees and their communities how many days notice of any closure or layoff affecting 50 or more full-time employees?
a. 50 days
b. 60 days
c. 70 days
d. 80 days

3 _______ 10. Personal freedom from unwarranted government or business intrusion into personal affairs involves
a. due process.
b. job expectancy rights.
c. rights of privacy.
d. performance evaluation.

3 _______ 11. Substance abusers
a. are five times more likely to file workers' comp claims.
b. are 33 percent less productive.
c. use 16 times as many health care benefits.
d. do all of the above.

3 _______ 12. Unless state or local laws either restrict or prohibit drug testing, in case of probable cause, private employers have a right to require employees to submit to a
a. polygraph test.
b. lie detector test.
c. psychiatric evaluation.
d. urinalysis or blood test.

3 _______ 13. It is not uncommon for employers to monitor the behavior of individual conduct in the workplace through
a. job evaluation.
b. job analysis.
c. equal pay for equal work.
d. surveillance techniques.

3 _______ 14. The method used discreetly by employers to discriminate against or stigmatize individuals applying for employment or individuals currently employed is
a. merit review.
b. genetic testing.
c. job security.
d. disciplinary action.

4 _______ 15. The primary responsibility for preventing or correcting disciplinary problems at the workplace rests with an employee's
a. top-line manager.
b. labor union.
c. immediate supervisor.
d. peers.

4 _______ 16. The foundation for an effective disciplinary system is composed of
a. organizational rules.
b. peer reviews.
c. alternative dispute resolutions.
d. employment-at-will principles.

4 _______ 17. An employee's right to representation during an investigative interview in a unionized organization is called
a. implied contract rights.
b. part of an open-door policy.
c. a peer-review system.
d. Weingarten rights

5 _______ 18. An essential part of an effective disciplinary system is an
a. implied contract.
b. accurate and complete set of work records.
c. outplacement service.
d. express contract.

5 _______ 19. To make sure employees are fully aware of the offense and before any disciplinary action is initiated, the supervisor should conduct a(n)
a. job evaluation.
b. performance appraisal.
c. investigative interview.
d. job analysis.

6 _______ 20. If a thorough investigation shows that an employee has violated an organization rule, the supervisor should impose
a. due process.
b. oral warnings.
c. compensatory damages.
d. disciplinary action.

6 _______ 21. The two primary approaches to disciplinary action are
a. progressive and positive discipline.
b. peer reviews and open-door policies.
c. outplacement and ombudsman services.
d. employment-at-will and implied contracts.

6 _______ 22. An application of corrective measures by increasing degrees designed to motivate an employee to correct his or her misconduct voluntarily is
a. constructive discharge.
b. due process.
c. progressive discipline.
d. negative discipline.

6 _______ 23. The approach that focuses on the early correction of misconduct, with the employee taking total responsibility for resolving the problem, is
a. orientation and training.
b. job security.
c. positive discipline.
d. merit review.

6 _______ 24. When employees fail to conform to organizational rules and regulations, the final disciplinary action in many cases is a
a. peer review.
b. discharge.
c. verbal warning.
d. written reprimand.

6 _______ 25. An employee's right to present his or her position during a disciplinary action is
a. employment-at-will.
b. due process.
c. implied contract.
d. willful discharge.

7 _______ 26. The term used to describe the different types of employee complaint resolution procedures is
a. discipline.
b. employment-at-will principle.
c. business ethics.
d. alternative dispute resolution.

7 _______ 27. Listening to an employee's complaint and attempting to resolve it by mediating a solution between the employee and the supervisor is the function of a(n)
a. shop steward.
b. corporate executive.
c. ombudsman.
d. stockholder.

7 _______ 28. The process that is used primarily to resolve discrimination suits by private employers in areas of age, gender, sexual harassment, and race is
a. job evaluation.
b. arbitration.
c. mediation.
d. conciliation.

8 _______ 29. What can be defined as a set of standards of acceptable conduct and moral judgment?
a. social responsibility.
b. ethics
c. human resources planning.
d. job enlargement.

8 _______ 30. The ultimate goal of ethics training is to
a. create social responsibility.
b. treat employees in a fair and equitable manner.
c. implement human resources planning.
d. facilitate job enlargement.

True/False

Identify the following statements as True or False.

1 _______ 1. The U.S. Constitution guarantees that jobs are among the specific property rights of employers.

2 _______ 2. The principle of employment-at-will assumes employers are free to terminate the employment relationship at any time, and without notice, for any reason, no reason, or even a bad reason.

2 _______ 3. The significance of wrongful discharge suits is that they challenge the employer's right under the implied employment concept to bilaterally discharge employees.

3 _______ 4. Drug testing is most prevalent among employees in sensitive positions within the public sector, in organizations doing business with the federal government, and in public and private transportation outfits.

3 _______ 5. Employers subject to the Americans with Disabilities Act need not comply with the law's provisions regarding drug addiction.

3 _______ 6. Employees have limited expectation of privacy in places where work rules that provide for inspections have been put into effect; they do not have to comply with probable-cause searches by employers.

3 _______ 7. The information kept in an employee's personnel file does not have a significant impact, positive or negative, on career development.

3 _______ 8. The right to privacy does not extend to email and voice mail messages.

4 _______ 9. A major responsibility of the human resources department is to develop and to have top management approve its disciplinary policies and procedures.

5 _______ 10. When taken against employees, disciplinary action should always be thought of as punishment.

5 _______ 11. When preparing documentation, it is important for a manager to record the incident immediately after the infraction takes place, when the memory of it is still fresh, and to ensure that the record is complete and accurate.

5 _______ 12. The investigative interview should concentrate on how the offense violated the performance and behavior standards of the job.

5 _______ 13. An employee's right to representation in a unionized organization does not extend to all interviews with management and organized labor.

6 _______ 14. The sequence and severity of the disciplinary action vary with the type of offense and the circumstances surrounding it.

6 _______ 15. While positive discipline appears similar to progressive discipline, its emphasis is on giving employees reprimands rather than reminders as a way to improve performance.

6 _______ 16. The right of the employee to tell his or her side of the story regarding the alleged infraction of organizational rules is an employee assistance program.

7 _______ 17. A procedure that allows the employee to submit a complaint to successively higher levels of management is the step-review system.

7 _______ 18. The peer-review system can be used as the sole method for resolving employee complaints, or it can be used in conjunction with a step-review system.

7 _______ 19. Two of the major weaknesses of an open-door policy are the willingness of managers to listen honestly to employees and the willingness of workers to approach managers with their complaints.

7 _______ 20. Since the ombudsman has no authority to finalize a solution to the problem, compromises are highly possible and all concerned tend to feel satisfied with the outcome.

7 _______ 21. Mediation employs a neutral third party to assist employees and managers to reach a voluntary agreement unacceptable to both parties.

7 _______ 22. Arbitration agreements may prevent employees from suing their employer in court, and may preclude employees from filing discrimination charges with the Equal Employment Opportunity Commission.

8 _______ 23. Managers need not comply with governmental regulation to promote an environment free from litigation.

8 _______ 24. Compliance with laws and the behavioral treatment of employees are two completely different aspects of the manager's job.

8 _______ 25. Many organizations have their own code of ethics that governs relations with employees and the public at large.

Matching

Match each term with the proper definition.

Terms

a. alternative dispute resolution (ADR)
b. constructive discharge
c. discipline
d. due process
e. employee rights
f. employment-at-will principle
g. ethics
h. Weingarten rights
i. mediation
j. mediator
k. negligence
l. ombudsman
m. open-door policy
n. peer-review system
o. positive, or nonpunitive, discipline
p. progressive discipline system
q. psychological contract
r. step-review system
s. whistle blower

Definitions

_______ 1. application of corrective measures by increasing stages

_______ 2. system for reviewing employee complaints that utilizes a group composed of equal numbers of employee representatives and management appointees, which functions as a jury since its members weigh evidence, consider arguments, and, after deliberation, vote independently to render a final decision

_______ 3. failure to provide reasonable care where such failure results in injury to consumers or other employees

_______ 4. technique applied to different types of employee complaint or dispute-resolution procedures

_______ 5. the use of an impartial neutral party to reach a compromise decision in employment disputes

_______ 6. employee's right to present his or her position during a disciplinary action

_______ 7. system of discipline that focuses on the early correction of employee misconduct, with the employee taking total responsibility for correcting the problem

_______ 8. policy of settling grievances that identifies various levels of management above the immediate supervisor for employee contact

_______ 9. the right of an employer to fire an employee without giving a reason and the right of an employee to quit when he or she chooses

_______ 10. system for reviewing employee complaints and disputes by successively higher levels of management

_______ 11. definitions include (1) treatment that punishes; (2) orderly behavior in an organizational setting; or (3) training that molds and strengthens desirable conduct or corrects undesirable conduct and develops self-control

_______ 12. designated individual from whom employees may seek counsel for the resolution of their complaints

_______ 13. guarantees of fair treatment from employers, particularly regarding an employee's right to privacy

_______ 14. employee's right to representation during an investigative interview in a unionized organization.

_______ 15. set of standards of conduct and moral judgments that help to determine right and wrong behavior

_______ 16. an employee voluntarily terminating his or her employment because of harsh, unreasonable employment conditions placed upon the individual by the employer

_______ 17. expectations of a fair exchange of employment obligations between an employee and employer

_______ 18. employee who complains to governmental agencies about his or her employer's illegal or immoral acts or illegal practices

_______ 19. third party in an employment dispute who meets with one party and then the other in order to suggest compromise solutions or recommend concessions from each side

Internet Exercises

When can constructive discharge be upheld?
http://www.legalworkplace.com/termination/constructive-discharge.aspx

What is an employee bill of rights?
http://www.findarticles.com/p/articles/mi_m0MNT/is_4_57/ai_99932979.

How to Develop and Utilize Ethical Codes in the Business World

Ethical codes are extremely relevant especially when working in an organization that is customer driven. For example, IBM's mission is to be customer-driven to create consumer satisfaction at all costs. When joining an organization, you must have orientation and training on ethical codes, policies, and procedures.
Ethics can be defined as a set of standards of acceptable conduct and moral judgment. Ethics provides cultural guidelines, organizational or societal, that help decide between proper and improper conduct. Ethics in human resources management extends beyond the legal requirements of managing employees. Managers engage in ethical behavior when employees are treated in an objective and fair way and when an employee's personal and work-related rights are respected and valued.

Organizations have ethics committees to provide training to employees. The ultimate goals of ethics training are to avoid unethical behavior and adverse publicity and to gain a strategic advantage but most of all, to treat employees in a fair and equitable manner, recognizing them as productive members of the organization.

SOLUTIONS

Multiple Choice:	True/False:	Matching:
1. a	1. False	1. p
2. c	2. True	2. n
3. c	3. False	3. k
4. c	4. True	4. a
5. b	5. False	5. i
6. c	6. False	6. d
7. d	7. False	7. o
8. b	8. True	8. m
9. b	9. True	9. f
10. c	10. False	10. r
11. d	11. True	11. c

12. d
13. d
14. b
15. c
16. a
17. d
18. b
19. c
20. d
21. a
22. c
23. c
24. b
25. b
26. d
27. c
28. b
29. b
30. b

12. True
13. True
14. True
15. False
16. False
17. True
18. True
19. False
20. True
21. False
22. False
23. False
24. True
25. True

12. l
13. e
14. h
15. g
16. b
17. q
18. s
19. j

False Statements Made True

1. The U.S. Constitution **carries no mandate that** guarantees that jobs are among the specific property rights of employers.
3. The significance of wrongful discharge suits is that they challenge the employer's right under the **employment-at-will** concept to bilaterally discharge employees.
5. Employers subject to the Americans with Disabilities Act **must** comply with the law's provisions regarding drug addiction.
6. Employees have limited **reasonable** expectation of privacy in places where work rules that provide for inspections have been put into effect; they **must** comply with probable-cause searches by employers.
7. The information kept in an employee's personnel file **can** have a significant impact, positive or negative, on career development.
10. When taken against employees, disciplinary action should **never** be thought of as punishment.
15. While positive discipline appears similar to progressive discipline, its emphasis is on giving employees **reminders** rather than **reprimands** as a way to improve performance.
16. The right of the employee to tell his or her side of the story regarding the alleged infraction of organizational rules is **due process**.

19. Two of the major weaknesses of an open-door policy are the **unwillingness** of managers to listen honestly to employees and the **reluctance** of workers to approach managers with their complaints.
21. Mediation employs a neutral third party to assist employees and managers to reach a voluntary agreement **acceptable** to both parties.
22. Arbitration agreements may prevent employees from suing their employer in court; **they cannot** preclude employees from filing discrimination charges with the Equal Employment Opportunity Commission.
23. Managers **must** comply with governmental regulation to promote an environment free from litigation.

CHAPTER

14

THE DYNAMICS OF LABOR RELATIONS

Workers unionize so they can influence employer decisions affecting their employment conditions and general welfare. When employees are unionized, human resources policies can no longer be determined unilaterally by the employer. Instead, these policies and practices are subject to the terms of the labor agreement that has been negotiated with the union. A major responsibility of the local union officers is to ensure that these terms are observed and that the rights of members provided by the agreement are protected. Labor agreements, which determine conditions of employment for union members, are achieved through collective bargaining. Bargaining success depends not only on the skills of the negotiators but also on the power each side can exercise to support its bargaining demands. Once the contract is ratified, its terms and conditions of employment bind both parties until it is renegotiated. During the period the contract is in force, the parties learn to cooperate through the administration of the agreement. When conflict arises over the rights the contract grants to each side, the grievance/arbitration provisions of the contract are invoked to resolve these differences.

LEARNING OBJECTIVES

After studying this chapter, you should be able to

1. Identify and explain the principal federal laws that provide the framework for labor relations.

2. Explain the reasons employees join unions.

3. Describe the process by which unions organize employees and gain recognition as their bargaining agent.

4. Discuss the bargaining process and the bargaining goals and strategies of a union and an employer.

5. Differentiate the forms of bargaining power that a union and an employer may utilize to enforce their bargaining demands.

6 Describe a typical union grievance procedure and explain the basis for arbitration awards.

7 Discuss some of the contemporary challenges to labor organizations.

CHAPTER SUMMARY RELATING TO LEARNING OBJECTIVES

1 The Railway Labor Act (1926) affords collective bargaining rights to workers employed in the railway and airline industries. The Norris-LaGuardia Act (1932) imposes limitations on the granting of injunctions in labor-management disputes. Most private employees are granted representation rights through the Wagner Act (1935), which has helped protect and encourage union organizing and bargaining activities. The passage of the Taft-Hartley Act (1947) and the Landrum-Griffin Act (1959) has served to establish certain controls over the internal affairs of unions and their relations with employers.

2 Studies show that workers unionize for different economic, psychological, and social reasons. While some employees may join unions because they are required to do so, most belong to unions because they are convinced that unions help them to improve their wages, benefits, and various working conditions. Employee unionization is largely caused by dissatisfaction with managerial practices and procedures.

3 A formal union organizing campaign is used to solicit employee support for the union. Once employees demonstrate their desire to unionize through signing authorization cards, the union will petition the National Labor Relations Board (NLRB) for a secret-ballot election. If 51 percent of those voting in the election vote for the union, the NLRB will certify the union as the bargaining representative for all employees in the bargaining unit.

4 Negotiating a labor agreement is a detailed process. Each side will prepare a list of proposals it wishes to achieve while additionally trying to anticipate those proposals desired by the other side. Bargaining teams must be selected, and all proposals must be analyzed to determine their impact on and cost to the organization. Both employer and union negotiators are sensitive to current bargaining patterns within the industry, general cost-of-living trends, and geographical wage differentials. Managers establish goals that seek to retain control over operations and to minimize costs. Union negotiators focus their demands around improved wages, hours, and working conditions. An agreement is reached when both sides compromise their original positions and final terms fall within the limits of the parties' bargaining zone. Traditionally, collective bargaining between labor and management has been

adversarial. Presently, there is an increased interest in nonadversarial negotiations—negotiations based on mutual gains and a heightened respect between the parties. What the Federal Mediation and Conciliation Service (FMCS) calls interest-based bargaining (IBB) is one form of nonadversarial negotiation.

5 The collective bargaining process includes not only the actual negotiations but also the power tactics used to support negotiating demands. When negotiations become deadlocked, bargaining becomes a power struggle to force from either side the concessions needed to break the deadlock. The union's power in collective bargaining comes from its ability to picket, strike, or boycott the employer. The employer's power during negotiation comes from its ability to lock out employees or to operate during a strike by using managerial or replacement employees.

6 When differences arise between labor and management they are normally resolved through the grievance procedure. Grievance procedures are negotiated and thus reflect the needs and desires of the parties. The typical grievance procedure will consist of three, four, or five steps, each step having specific filing and reply times. Higher-level managers and union officials will become involved in disputes at the higher steps of the grievance procedure. The final step of the grievance procedure may be arbitration. Arbitrators will render a final decision to problems not resolved at lower grievance steps.

The submission agreement is a statement of the issue to be solved through arbitration. It is simply the problem the parties wish to have settled. The arbitrator must answer the issue by basing the arbitration award on four factors: the contents of the labor agreement (or employment policy), the submission agreement as written, testimony and evidence obtained at the hearing, and various arbitration standards developed over time to assist in the resolution of different types of labor-management disputes. Arbitration is not an exact science, because arbitrators will give varying degrees of importance to the evidence and criteria by which disputes are resolved.

7 Challenges facing union leaders today include declining membership caused by technological advancements and increased domestic and global competition. Labor organizations experience less success in organizations where employers establish progressive HR policies in the areas of wages, employee benefits, and organizaional policies that enhance job security and the dignity of employees. To counteract a declining membership base, unions have become aggressive in organizing employees in lower-skilled occupations, recent immigrants, and employees in white-collar jobs. Through union mergers and coalitions, labor organizations seek to become more effective in their organizing efforts.

REVIEW QUESTIONS

Multiple Choice

Choose the letter of the word or phrase that best completes each statement.

1 _______ 1. The act that severely restricted the ability of employers to obtain an injunction forbidding a union from engaging in peaceful picketing, boycotts, or various striking activities is the
a. Taft-Hartley Act.
b. Wagner Act.
c. Norris-LaGuardia Act.
d. Landrum-Griffin Act.

1 _______ 2. The agency responsible for administering and enforcing the Wagner Act is the
a. Affirmative Action Committee.
b. Equal Employment Opportunity Commission.
c. Occupational Safety and Health Administration.
d. National Labor Relations Board.

1 _______ 3. Union self-organizing activities and collective bargaining were legalized through the
a. Wagner Act.
b. Taft-Hartley Act.
c. Norris-LaGuardia Act.
d. Landrum-Griffin Act.

1 _______ 4. Section 8 of which act lists unfair labor practices of employers?
a. Wagner Act.
b. Taft-Hartley Act.
c. Norris-LaGuardia Act.
d. Landrum-Griffin Act.

1 _______ 5. Which act lists unfair labor practices of unions?
a. Wagner Act.
b. Taft-Hartley Act.
c. Norris-LaGuardia Act.
d. Landrum-Griffin Act.

1 _______ 6. The Landrum-Griffin Act of 1959 states that every union member has been given the following rights, *except*
a. nominating candidates for union office.
b. voting in union elections or referendums.
c. attending union meetings.
d. creating featherbedding.

2 _______ 7. A provision of the labor agreement that requires employees to join the union as a requirement for their employment is called
a. management prerogatives.
b. closed ship.
c. agency shop.
d. union shop.

2 _______ 8. The strongest reasons to join a labor union are the traditional issues of dissatisfaction with wages, benefits, and
a. management prerogatives.
b. working conditions.
c. compulsory arbitration.
d. job design.

2 _______ 9. When employees perceive that managerial practices regarding promotion, transfer, shift assignment, or other job-related policies are administered in an unfair or biased manner, they may seek
a. decertification.
b. mediation.
c. unionization.
d. binding arbitration.

2 _______ 10. The major concerns for which employees join unions involve
a. social and leadership needs.
b. esteem and self-actualization.
c. job enlargement and enrichment.
d. achievement and physiological requirements.

3 _______ 11. Unions have been shocked into more aggressive and creative tactics in organizing strategies to counteract employer antiunion campaigns and to compensate for a(n)
a. closed-shop agreement.
b. decline in membership.
c. organizational picketing event.
d. wildcat strike.

3 ______ 12. Once the union is certified, the employer is obligated to begin negotiations leading toward a(n)
a. grievance.
b. wildcat strike.
c. authorization card.
d. labor agreement.

3 ______ 13. What percentage of employees within a bargaining unit must a union succeed in signing up, before thay can petition for an NLRB conducted election?
a. 30%
b. 40%
c. 50%
d. 60%

3 ______ 14. Unions seek greater participation in management decisions that involve such issues as subcontracting of work, productivity standards, and job content as a result of
a. job security.
b. management prerogatives.
c. working conditions.
d. hours of work.

3 ______ 15. In 2005, six unions split from the AFL-CIO to form
a. American Federation of Teachers
b. AFSCME
c. Change to Win
d. National Education Association.

3 ______ 16. To the "rank-and-file" union member, the importance of unionism resides in the activities of the
a. piece-rate systems.
b. management.
c. self-managed teams.
d. local union and its leaders.

4 ______ 17. In collective bargaining there are economic pressures in the form of lockouts, plant closures, and the replacement of strikers that are used by the
a. business agent.
b. labor union.
c. employer.
d. shop steward.

4 _______ 18. In collective bargaining, all matters concerning rates of pay, wages, hours of employment, or other conditions of employment are examples of
a. mandatory subjects.
b. voluntary issues.
c. illegal subjects.
d. unauthorized subjects.

4 _______ 19. Areas or subjects where management and labor are free to bargain but neither side can force the other side to bargain are
a. mandatory subjects.
b. involuntary issues.
c. illegal subjects.
d. permissive issues.

4 _______ 20. Illegal subjects in collective bargaining would include the closed-shop security agreement and
a. wages and salaries.
b. compulsory dues check-off.
c. working conditions.
d. hours of work.

4 _______ 21. The area within which the union and the employer are willing to concede when negotiating is called the
a. bargaining zone.
b. impasse zone.
c. management lockout.
d. wildcat strike.

5 _______ 22. The refusal of a group of employees to perform their jobs and withhold their services when negotiations become deadlocked is a
a. lockout.
b. boycott.
c. strike.
d. grievance procedure.

5 _______ 23. When a union asks its members or customers not to patronize a business where there is a labor dispute, it is asking for a
a. labor strike.
b. company lockout.
c. slowdown.
d. boycott.

5 _______ 24. Right –to-work laws ban
a. labor strike.
b. company lockout.
c. slowdown.
d. any from of compulsory union membership.

5 _______ 25. A third party that can be utilized to recommend a compromise when the disputing parties are unable to resolve their differences is called a
a. mediator.
b. negotiator.
c. business agent.
d. narrator.

5 _______ 26. An individual who has binding authority to resolve disputes arising in connection with the administration of an agreement is a(n)
a. mediator.
b. arbitrator.
c. business agent.
d. human resources director.

5 _______ 27. In the public sector, where strikes are largely prohibited, a common method used in the attempt to resolve bargaining deadlocks is
a. conciliation.
b. interest arbitration.
c. outsourcing.
d. performance appraisal.

6 _______ 28. Considered by some authorities to be the heart of the bargaining agreement, the safety valve that gives flexibility to the whole system of collective bargaining is the
a. arbitration panel.
b. primary boycott.
c. grievance procedure.
d. closed-shop security provision.

6 _______ 29. Unions have a legal obligation to provide assistance to members who are pursuing a grievance under the
a secondary boycott award.
b. employment-at-will doctrine.
c. closed-shop security provision.
d. fair representation doctrine.

7 _______ 30. The fastest-growing segment of working people as potent prospects for union growth are
a. professional employees.
b. craft employees.
c. self-managed teams.
d. immigrants.

True/False

Identify the following statements as True or False.

1 _______ 1. The primary purpose of the Railway Labor Act is to create the use of injunctions between labor and management.

1 _______ 2. Before an injunction may be issued, employers need not show that lack of an injunction will cause greater harm to the employer than to the union.

1 _______ 3. The Wagner Act created the National Labor Relations Board to govern labor relations in the United States.

1 _______ 4. Because of the high incidence of strikes after World War II, the Taft-Hartley Act created the Federal Mediation and Conciliation Service to help resolve negotiating disputes.

3 _______ 5. Most labor-organizing campaigns are undertaken by union organizers rather than employees.

3 _______ 6. At least 30 percent of the employees must sign authorization cards before the National Labor Relations Board will hold a representation election.

3 _______ 7. After the election is held, the winning party will be determined on the basis of the number of members of the bargaining unit.

3 _______ 8. The petition to hold representation elections is always initiated by the employer.

3 _______ 9. The center of power in the labor movement resides with national and international unions.

3 _______ 10. Depending on the size of the local union, one or more officers, in addition to the business representative, may be paid by the union to serve on a full-time basis.

3 _______ 11. Union stewards are normally elected by union members within their department and are always paid a union salary.

3 _______ 12. Business unionism is the general label given to the goals of American labor organizations: increased pay and benefits, job security, and improved working conditions.

3 _______ 13. Most state legislatures have granted public employees the right to strike.

4 _______ 14. Negotiators for an employer should develop a written plan called a proposal, which includes the collective bargaining strategy.

4 _______ 15. The initial meeting of the bargaining teams is a particularly important one because it establishes the climate that will prevail during the negotiations that follow.

4 _______ 16. Once bargaining begins, an employer is not obligated to negotiate in good faith with the union's representative over conditions of employment.

5 _______ 17. When negotiations become deadlocked, the employer's bargaining power largely rests on being able to continue operations in the face of a strike or to shut down operations entirely.

5 _______ 18. If employees decide to strike the organization, employers have the right to hire replacement workers.

5 _______ 19. A mediator assumes the role of a decision maker and determines what the settlement between the two parties should be.

6 _______ 20. If a grievance cannot be resolved through the grievance procedure, each disputing party must decide whether to use arbitration to resolve the case.

6 _______ 21. A grievance should be viewed as something to be won or lost from the perspective of the government.

6 _______ 22. The arbitration hearing process begins with the swearing-in of witnesses and the introduction of the submission agreement, which is a statement of the problem to be resolved.

6 _______ 23. The arbitration award should include not only the arbitrator's decision but also the rationale for it.

6 _______ 24. Arbitrators are essentially constrained to decide cases based on the wording of the labor agreement but never to the facts, testimony, and evidence presented at the hearing.

7 _______ 25. Targeted prospects for union growth include low-wage service workers on the bottom tier of the U.S. economy and recent immigrants who are working.

Matching

Match each term with the proper definition.

Terms

a. arbitrator
b. authorization card
c. bargaining power
d. bargaining unit
e. bargaining zone
f. business unionism
g. collective bargaining process
h. craft unions
i. employee associations
j. exclusive representation
k. fair-representation doctrine
l. grievance procedure
m. industrial union
n. interest-based bargaining
o. labor relations process
p. rights arbitration
q. unfair labor practices (ULPs)
r. union shop
s. union steward

Definitions

_______ 1. specific employer and union illegal practices that operate to deny employees their rights and benefits under federal labor law

_______ 2. unions that represent skilled craft workers

_______ 3. a statement signed by an employee authorizing a union to act as a representative of the employee for purposes of collective bargaining

_______ 4. employee who as a nonpaid union official represents the interests of members in their relations with management

_______ 5. logical sequence of four events: (1) workers desire collective representation, (2) union begins its organizing campaign, (3) collective negotiations lead to a contract, and (4) the contract is administered

_______ 6. term applied to the goals of U.S. labor organizations, which collectively bargain for improvements in wages, hours, job security, and working conditions

_______ 7. labor organizations that represent various groups of professional and white-collar employees in labor-management relations

_______ 8. provision of the labor agreement that requires employees to join the union as a condition of their employment

_______ 9. unions that represent all workers—skilled, semiskilled, unskilled—employed along industry lines

_______ 10. group of two or more employees who share common employment interests and conditions and may reasonably be grouped together for purposes of collective bargaining

_______ 11. formal procedure that provides for the union to represent members and nonmembers in processing a grievance

_______ 12. doctrine under which unions have a legal obligation to provide assistance to both members and nonmembers in labor relations matters

_______ 13. arbitration over interpretation of the meaning of contract terms or employee work grievances

_______ 14. process of negotiating a labor agreement, including the use of economic pressures by both parties

_______ 15. neutral third party who resolves a labor dispute by issuing a final decision in the disagreement

_______ 16. problem-solving bargaining based on a win-win philosophy and the development of a positive long-term relationship

_______ 17. the power of labor and management to achieve their goals through economic, social, or political influence

_______ 18. the legal right and responsibility of the union to represent all bargaining unit members equally regardless of whether employees join the union or not

_______ 19. area within which the union and the employer are willing to concede when bargaining

Internet Exercise

How can the arbitration process be expedited?
http://www.findarticles.com/p/articles/mi_qa3923/is_200305/ai_n9282717.

How to Manage a Nonunion Operation

Managing a nonunion operation is paramount for the success of an organization.

Management must create an environment of openness, trust, and respect for the firm's employees. Managers must demonstrate a clear appreciation of their employees and permit them to experience a high degree of job satisfaction. A management style that challenges employees and establishes high expectations for their work is essential. Creating a closely knit culture among management and employees is recommended. Employee empowerment will permit decision making to take place closest to the point of action. To keep a union out, employee needs must be identified and met. Management must offer extrinsic and intrinsic rewards to employees. Extrinsic rewards include money, bonuses, and other financial incentives. Intrinsic rewards include recognition, self-esteem, and self-actualizing experiences. The ultimate goal is for employees to be challenged to develop to their fullest potential. These recommendations will assist management to create and maintain a union-free environment.

SOLUTIONS

Multiple Choice:	True/False:	Matching:
1. c	1. False	1. q
2. d	2. False	2. h
3. a	3. True	3. b
4. a	4. True	4. s
5. b	5. False	5. o
6. d	6. True	6. f
7. d	7. False	7. i
8. b	8. False	8. r
9. c	9. True	9. m
10. a	10. True	10. d
11. b	11. False	11. l
12. d	12. True	12. k
13. a	13. False	13. p
14. b	14. True	14. g
15. c	15. True	15. a
16. d	16. False	16. n
17. c	17. True	17. c
18. a	18. True	18. j
19. d	19. False	19. e
20. b	20. True	
21. a	21. False	
22. c	22. True	
23. d	23. True	
24. d	24. False	
25. a	25. True	
26. b		

27. b
28. c
29. d
30. d

False Statements Made True

1. The primary purpose of the Railway Labor Act is to **avoid service interruptions resulting from disputes between railroads and their operating unions**.
2. Before an injunction may be issued, employers **must** show that lack of an injunction will cause greater harm to the employer than to the union.
5. Most labor-organizing campaigns are undertaken by **employees rather than union organizers**.
7. After the election is held, the winning party will be determined on the basis of the **number of actual votes, not the number of members of the bargaining unit**.
8. The petition to hold representation elections is **usually** initiated by the **union**.
11. Union stewards are normally elected by union members within their department and **serve without union pay**.
13. Most state legislatures **have not** granted public employees the right to strike.
16. Once bargaining begins, an employer **is obligated** to negotiate in good faith with the union's representative over conditions of employment.
19. **An arbitrator** assumes the role of a decision maker and determines what the settlement between the two parties should be.
21. A grievance **should not** be viewed as something to be won or lost from the perspective of the government.
24. Arbitrators are essentially constrained to decide cases based on the wording of the labor agreement, **including** the facts, testimony, and evidence presented at the hearing.

PART SIX

Expanding Human Resources Management Horizons

CHAPTER 15

INTERNATIONAL HUMAN RESOURCES MANAGEMENT

A large percentage of the corporations in the United States are engaged in international business. Many of them are multinational corporations (MNCs) and thus have extensive facilities and human resources in foreign countries. The management of MNCs poses special problems. The cultural environment in which MNCs operate is especially important, and managers must be selected carefully and then trained to be effective in a specific environment. Differences among countries in the performance of HRM functions are reviewed briefly as a background for further study.

LEARNING OBJECTIVES

After studying this chapter, you should be able to

1. Identify the types of organizational forms used for competing internationally.
2. Explain the economic, political-legal, and cultural factors in different countries that HR managers need to consider.
3. Explain how domestic and international HRM differ.
4. Discuss the staffing process for individuals working internationally.
5. Identify the unique training needs for international assignees and their employees.
6. Identify the characteristics of a good international compensation plan.

7 Reconcile the difficulties of home- and host-country performance appraisals.

8 Explain how labor relations differ around the world.

CHAPTER SUMMARY RELATING TO LEARNING OBJECTIVES

1 There are four basic ways to organize for global competition: (1) The international corporation is essentially a domestic firm that has leveraged its existing capabilities to penetrate overseas markets; (2) the multinational corporation has fully autonomous units operating in multiple countries in order to address local issues; (3) the global corporation has a worldview but controls all international operations from its home office; and (4) the transnational corporation uses a network structure to balance global and local concerns.

2 In addition to economic considerations, political-legal and cultural factors in different parts of the world make some countries more desirable to do business with than others.

3 International HRM places greater emphasis on a number of responsibilities and functions such as relocation, orientation, and translation services to help employees adapt to a new and different environment outside their own country.

4 Many factors must be considered in the selection and development of employees. Though hiring host-country nationals or third-country nationals automatically avoids many potential problems, expatriates are preferable, but more costly, in some circumstances. When expatriates are hired, most companies try to minimize their stay. Operations are handed off to host-country nationals as soon as possible.

5 Once an expatriate is selected, an intensive training and development program is essential to qualify that person and his or her spouse for the assignment. Wherever possible, development should extend beyond information and orientation training to include sensitivity training and field experiences that will enable the manager to understand cultural differences better. Those in charge of the international program should provide the help needed to protect managers from career development risks, reentry problems, and culture shock. E-mail, instant messaging, and videoconferencing are making it easier for companies to stay in touch with their expatriates

6 Compensation systems should support the overall strategic intent of the organization but be customized for local conditions. For expatriates, compensation plans must provide an incentive to leave the United States; meet standard of living, health care, and safety needs; provide for the education of children, if necessary; and facilitate repatriation.

7 Although home-country managers frequently have formal responsibility for individuals on foreign assignment, they may not be able to fully understand expatriate experiences because geographical distances pose severe communication problems. Host-country managers may be in the best position to observe day-to-day performance but may be biased by cultural factors and may not have an overall view of the country. Performance evaluations should combine the two sources of appraisal information.

8 In many European countries (Germany, for example), employee representation is established by law. Organizations typically negotiate the agreement with the union at a national level, frequently with government intervention. In other countries, union activity is prohibited or limited to only large companies. European unions have much more political power than many other unions around the world, although their power has declined somewhat, due to globalization forces. The International Confederation of Free Trade Unions (IDFTU), the European Trade Union Confederation (ETUC), and the International Labor Organization (ILO) are among the major worldwide organizations endeavoring to improve the conditions of workers.

REVIEW QUESTIONS

Multiple Choice

Choose the letter of the word or phrase that best completes each statement.

1

_______ 1. A multinational firm that maintains control of operations back in the home office can be viewed as a
a. domestic corporation.
b. global corporation.
c. polycentric organization.
d. geocentric organization.

1

_______ 2. The type of organization that attempts to achieve the local responsiveness of a multinational corporation while also achieving the efficiencies of a global firm is a(n)
a. domestic business.
b. global business.
c. transnational corporation.
d. international organization.

2

_______ 3. Communications, religion, values and ideologies, education, and the social structure of a country are examples of
a. a cultural environnent.
b. an economic environnent.
c. employee and customer rights.
d. a physical environment.

2

_______ 4. The country in which an international business operates is the
a. third-world country.
b. domestic country.
c. home country.
d. host country.

4

_______ 5. Natives of a country other than the home country or the host country are
a. home-country nationals.
b. expatriates.
c. third-country nationals.
d. all of the above.

4 _______ 6. The following are different sources of employees with whom to staff international operations, *except*
a. preferential union shops.
b. home-country nationals.
c. host-country nationals.
d. third-country nationals.

4 _______ 7. Natives of the host country who manage international operations are known as
a. expatriate managers.
b. third-country nationals.
c. global managers.
d. host-country nationals.

4 _______ 8. A document issued by a government granting authority to a foreign individual to seek employment in that government's country is a
a. contract.
b. work permit or visa.
c. passport.
d. green card.

4 _______ 9. Compared to the United States, employee recruitment in other countries is subject to
a. management rights.
b. management prerogatives.
c. more government regulation.
d. marketing myopia practices.

4 _______ 10. A major source of trained labor in European nations is
a. apprenticeship training programs.
b. translation programs.
c. job analysis programs.
d. orientation programs.

4 _______ 11. Foreign workers invited to come to a country to perform needed labor are usually referred to as
a. human resources specialists.
b. operative employees.
c. guest workers.
d. immigrants.

4 _______ 12. The assembly of people of multiple nationalities who can work together effectively on projects that span multiple countries is a
a. trade agreement.
b. domestic work group.
c. cartel arrangement.
d. transnational team.

4 _______ 13. One of the principal causes of failure among employees working internationally is a lack of
a. assessment centers.
b. interviews.
c. tests.
d. training.

4 _______ 14. The most prevalent reasons for failure among expatriates working in foreign countries are
a. technical limitations.
b. family and lifestyle issues.
c. economic issues.
d. religious beliefs.

5 _______ 15. Most executives agree that the biggest problem for the foreign business traveler is
a. exchange rate conversion.
b. communicating in different languages.
c. strategic planning.
d. accepting bribes.

5 _______ 16. Managerial attitudes and behaviors are influenced by the society in which managers have
a. job evaluation.
b. received their education and training.
c. performance appraisals.
d. job analysis backgrounds.

5 _______ 17. Studying cultural differences can be helpful to managers in identifying and understanding cultural
a. augmented skills and the balance-sheet approach.
b. core skills and guest workers.
c. work attitudes and motivation.
d. work permits and work certificates.

5 _______ 18. A disorientation that causes perpetual stress experienced by people who settle overseas for extended periods is
a. culture shock.
b. culture environnent.
c. foreign exchange.
d. social culture disease.

5 _______ 19. Helping employees make the transition back home is
a. life-planning.
b. localization.
c. debriefing.
d. repatriation.

5 _______ 20. According to a recent survey, what percentage of expatriates believed that their careers had not advanced after returning home?
a. 40
b. 50
c. 60
d. 70

6 _______ 21. To be effective, an international compensation program must
a. provide an incentive to leave the United States.
b. facilitate reentry home.
c. be in writing.
d. do all of the above.

6 _______ 22. A compensation system designed to equal the purchasing power in a person's home country is a
a. job analysis program.
b. balance-sheet approach to management.
c. job description.
d. job specification.

6 _______ 23. Under which pay system, expatriates are given a portion of their pay in local currency to cover day-to-day expenses?
a. split-pay
b. balance-sheet approach.
c. Home-based pay
d. localization

6

_______ 24. Compensation that is equivalent to that earned by employees in the country where the expatriate is assigned is
a. a COLA.
b. incentive pay.
c. host-based pay.
d. home-based pay.

7

_______ 25. Because expatiate assignments are very costly, many HR Managers are increasingly under pressure to calculate the
a. return on investment of these assignments.
b. retention costs of these assignments.
c. third-country national costs of these assignments.
d. replacement costs of these assignments.

7

_______ 26. Although the home-country and host-country superiors may tell an expatriate how well he or she is doing, it is also important for expatriates to provide feedback regarding
a. the support they are receiving.
b. obstacles they face.
c. suggestions they have about the assignment.
d. all of the above.

8

_______ 27. Which country only has one union?
a. China
b. India
c. Japan
d. South Korea

8

_______ 28. The most active of the international union organizations has been the
a. International Confederation of Free Trade Unions.
b. All-China Federation of Trade Unions.
c. International Trade Corporation.
d. Global Union.

8

_______ 29. Which of the following organizations has had the greatest impact on the rights of workers throughout the world?
a. International Confederation of Free Trade Unions.
b. All-China Federation of Trade Unions.
c. International Trade Corporation.
d. International Labor Organization.

8 _______ 30. A higher form of worker participation in management is found in Germany where representation of labor by directors of a company is required by law. This arrangement is known as
a. codetermination.
b. joint venturing.
c. legitimate power.
d. self-managed teams.

True/False

Identify the following statements as True or False.

1 _______ 1. The international corporation is essentially a domestic firm that builds on its existing capabilities to penetrate home markets.

1 _______ 2. To balance a "global/local" dilemma, a transnational corporation uses a network structure that coordinates specialized facilities positioned around the world.

3 _______ 3. International HRM is the same as domestic HRM in all aspects.

3 _______ 4. All large corporations have a part-time staff of human resources specialists devoted to assisting in the globalization process.

4 _______ 5. Third-country nationals are natives of a country other than the home country or the host country.

4 _______ 6. Recently there has been a trend to use only expatriates in the lower management positions.

4 _______ 7. Employee recruitment in the United States is subject to more government regulation than in other countries.

4 _______ 8. The employment of nonnationals throughout the globe may involve lower direct labor costs.

4 _______ 9. In the United States, managers tend to emphasize seniority, with the most-senior person getting the job.

4 _______ 10. One way to improve the success of expatriate assignments is to involve spouses early in the process.

4 _______ 11. Core skills are considered critical to an employee's success abroad.

4 _______ 12. The biggest mistake managers can make is to assume that people are different everywhere.

4 _______ 13. One of the greatest contributions that the United States has made to work organizations is in improving the competence of managers.

4 _______ 14. Working abroad tends to increase a person's responsibilities and influence within the organization.

5 _______ 15. When compared with the Japanese, Americans may feel more loyalty to their organizations.

5 _______ 16. One of the important dimensions of leadership is the degree to which managers invite employee participation in decision making.

5 _______ 17. One of the most frequent causes of an employee's failure to complete an international assignment is personal and family stress.

5 _______ 18. Repatriation is the process of helping an employee make the transition back home from an international assignment.

5 _______ 19. All companies have career development programs designed for repatriating employees.

5 _______ 20. More companies are making an effort to keep in touch with expatriates while they are abroad, which has been easier with email, instant messaging, and videoconferencing.

6 _______ 21. One of the most complex areas of international HRM is compensation.

6 _______ 22. Host-country employees are generally paid on the basis of productivity, time spent on the job, or a combination of these factors.

7 _______ 23. HR Managers are increasingly under pressure to calculate the return on investment on expatriate assignments.

8 _______ 24. Because for most companies, labor is their largest cost, it plays a prime role in international HR decision making.

8 _______ 25. The collective bargaining process can vary widely among countries, especially with regard to the role that government plays.

Matching

Match each term with the proper definition.

Terms

a. augmented skills
b. balance-sheet approach
c. codetermination
d. core skills
e. cultural environment
f. culture shock
g. expatriates, home-country nationals
h. failure rate
i. global corporation
j. global manager
k. guest workers
l. host-based pay
m. home-based pay
n. host country
o. host-country nationals
p. international corporation
q. localization
r. multinational corporation (MNC)
s. repatriation
t. third-country nationals
u. transnational corporation
v. transnational teams
w. work permit or visa
x. global compensation system
y. split pay

Definitions

_______ 1. foreign workers invited into a foreign labor market to perform needed labor

_______ 2. perceptual stress experienced by people who settle overseas

_______ 3. firm with independent business units operating in multiple countries

_______ 4. skills helpful in facilitating the efforts of expatriate managers

_______ 5. natives of the host country

_______ 6. representation of labor on the board of directors of a company

_______ 7. firm that has integrated worldwide operations through a centralized home office

_______ 8. compensation system designed to match the purchasing power of a person's home country

_______ 9. government document granting a foreign individual the right to seek employment

_______ 10. country in which an international corporation operates

_______ 11. employees from the home country who are sent on international assignment

_______ 12. communication, religion, values and ideologies, education, and social structure of a country

_______ 13. domestic firm that uses its existing capabilities to move into overseas markets

_______ 14. teams composed of members of multiple nationalities working on projects that span multiple countries

_______ 15. skills considered critical in an employee's success abroad

_______ 16. firm that attempts to balance local responsiveness and global scale via a network of specialized operating units

_______ 17. manager equipped to run an international business

_______ 18. percentage of expatriates who do not perform satisfactorily

_______ 19. natives of a country other than the home country or the host country

_______ 20. process that helps employees make the transition back home after a foreign assignment

_______ 21. expatriate pay comparable to that earned by employees in a host country

_______ 22. pay based on an expatriate's home country's compensation practices

_______ 23. adapting pay and other compensation benefits to match that of a particular country

_______ 24. A centralized pay system whereby host-county employees are offered a full range of training programs, benefits, and pay comparable with a firm's domestic employee but adjusted for local differences

_______ 25. A system whereby expatriates are given a portion of their pay in the local currency to cover their day-to-day expenses and a portion of their pay in their home currency to safeguard their earnings from changes in inflation or foreign exchange rates.

Internet Exercises

How can you bridge the gap to minimize culture shock?
http://www.findarticles.com/p/articles/mi_m0DTI/is_7_31/ai_104079169.
What are the challenges of international human resources management?
http://www.findarticles.com/p/articles/mi_m3495/is_n3_v42/ai_19445784.

How to Prepare for an International Assignment for a Multinational Corporation

In the recruiting and selection process for an international assignment, you should understand the preparation required for this opportunity. This would include an understanding of the host nation's culture, political and legal framework, and customs. Once selected, you should undertake an intensive training and development program. Development should extend beyond information and orientation training to include sensitivity training and field experiences that will enable you to better understand cultural differences. Seek the support of the person(s) in charge of the international program in order to avoid career development risks, reentry problems, and culture shock.

The socialization process involving the culture and customs is an important orientation objective. To understand fully the challenges of the international assignment, you should be able to adapt to the methodology of the foreign country's business practices. Finally, do not impose American values and business practices in the foreign country. Preparation includes understanding the business customs and practices that exist in the foreign culture.

SOLUTIONS

Multiple Choice:	True/False:	Matching:
1. b	1. False	1. k
2. c	2. True	2. f
3. a	3. False	3. r
4. d	4. False	4. a
5. c	5. True	5. o
6. a	6. False	6. c
7. d	7. False	7. i
8. b	8. True	8. b
9. c	9. False	9. w
10. a	10. True	10. n
11. c	11. True	11. g
12. d	12. False	12. e
13. d	13. True	13. p
14. b	14. True	14. v
15. b	15. False	15. d
16. b	16. True	16. u
17. c	17. True	17. j
18. a	18. True	18. h
19. d	19. False	19. t
20. c	20. True	20. s
21. d	21. True	21. l
22. b	22. True	22. m
23. a	23. True	23. q
24. c	24. True	24. x
25. a	25. True	25. y
26 d.		
27. a		
28. a		
29. d		
30. a		

False Statements Made True

1. The international corporation is essentially a domestic firm that builds on its existing capabilities to penetrate **overseas** markets.
3. International HRM **differs from** domestic HRM in **many ways**.
4. **Most** large corporations have a **full-time** staff of human resources **managers** devoted to assisting in the globalization process.
6. Recently there has been a trend to use only expatriates in the **top** management positions.
7. Employee recruitment in the United States is subject to **less** government regulation than in other countries.
9. In the United States, managers tend to emphasize **merit**, with the **best-qualified** person getting the job.
12. The biggest mistake managers can make is to assume that people are **the same** everywhere.
15. When compared with the Japanese, Americans may feel **little** loyalty to their organizations.
19. **Unfortunately, not all** companies have career development programs designed for repatriating employees.

CHAPTER

16 CREATING HIGH-PERFORMANCE WORK SYSTEMS

High-performance work systems are integral for HR practices that maximize employee knowledge, skill, commitment, and flexibility. The system begins with implementing empowered work teams to perform key business processes. Training of team members is paramount, and reward systems are used to motivate behavior. When the subsystems complement one another, the result is both an internal and external fit that produces a holistic system. For the system to function effectively, it must have top management as well as labor union support. The result is a high-performance work system that benefits both the employees and the organization.

LEARNING OBJECTIVES

After studying this chapter, you should be able to

1. Discuss the underlying principles of high-performance work systems.
2. Identify the components that make up a high-performance work system.
3. Describe how the components fit together and support strategy.
4. Recommend processes for implementing high-performance work systems.
5. Discuss the outcomes for both employees and the organization.

CHAPTER SUMMARY RELATING TO LEARNING OBJECTIVES

1 High-performance work systems are specific combinations of HR practices, work structures, and processes that maximize employee knowledge, skill, commitment, and flexibility. They are based on contemporary principles of high-involvement organizations. These principles include shared information, knowledge development, performance-reward linkages, egalitarianism, and employee engagement.

2 High-performance work systems are composed of several interrelated components. Team members are carefully selected and undergo extensive training, including cross training, and often share leadership duties. Typically, the system begins with designing empowered work teams to carry out key business processes. Integrated information technology systems can help ensure that employees have the information they need to make timely and productive decisions. To align the interests of employees with those of the organization, the reward systems associated with high-performance work systems are performance based, and often include group and organizational incentive pay, and sometimes skill-based pay.

3 The pieces of the system are important only in terms of how they help the entire system function. When all the pieces support and complement one another, high-performance work systems achieve internal fit. When the system is aligned with the competitive priorities of the organization as a whole, it achieves external fit as well.

4 Implementing high-performance work systems within existing organizations often has to be done in stages. The implementation is much more likely to go smoothly if a business case is first made for the HPWS and fully communicated to employees. The support of the firm's top-managers is critical, and so too is the support of union representatives and the company's other key groups and divisions. Because firms today gain a competitive advantage primarily from the capabilities of the talent, a company's HR department can be an invaluable partner when it comes to implementing a HPWS. HR personnel can also help establish a transition structure to shepherd the implementation through its various stages and reassure employees they will be successful working in the new system. Once the system is in place, it should be evaluated in terms of its processes, outcomes, sustainability, and ongoing fit with strategic objectives of the organization.

5 Progressive organizations of all sizes have successfully implemented high-performance work systems. When implemented effectively, high-performance work systems benefit both employees and their organizations. Employees become more engaged and empowered to make decisions, experience greater career growth and satisfaction, and become more valuable contributors to their firms. Organizations benefit from higher productivity, quality, flexibility, and customer satisfaction. These features together can provide a company with a sustainable competitive advantage.

REVIEW QUESTIONS

Multiple Choice

Choose the letter of the word or phrase that best completes each statement.

1 _______ 1. The specific combination of human resources practices, work structures, and processes that maximize employee knowledge, skill, commitment, and flexibility is known as
   a. high-performance work systems.
   b. labor-intensive organizations.
   c. self-managed teams.
   d. external integration.

1 _______ 2. One of the primary principles that support high-performance work systems is
   a. job turnover linkage.
   b. complacency evolution.
   c. sharing information.
   d. employment transfer linkage.

1 _______ 3. The principle that includes selecting the best and the brightest candidates available in the labor market and providing all employees opportunities to continuously hone their talents is
   a. shared information.
   b. egalitarianism.
   c. knowledge development.
   d. external fit.

1 _______ 4. Involving employees in decision making and giving them the power to act tends to increase what HR professionals refer to as
a. shared information.
b. employee engagement
c. knowledge development.
d. external fit.

1 _______ 5. When employees pursue outcomes that are mutually beneficial to themselves and the organization, this process is known as the
a. job-knowledge linkage.
b. performance-reward linkage.
c. principle of egalitarianism.
d. concept of shared information.

1 _______ 6. The concept that eliminates status and power differences and, in the process, increases collaboration and teamwork is
a. shared information.
b. performance-reward linkage.
c. knowledge development.
d. egalitarianism.

1 _______ 7. Moving power downward in organizations • by empowering employees • frequently requires
a. structural changes.
b. bureaucratic changes.
c. centralized instruction.
d. cross-training.

2 _______ 8. Emphasis on teamwork, involvement, and continuous improvement requires that employees develop a broader understanding of work processes performed by others around them rather than rely on just knowing their own jobs through
a. corporate downsizing.
b. internal fit.
c. cross-training.
d. external fit.

2 _______ 9. High-performance work systems frequently begin with the way
a. work is designed.
b. people are hired.
c. employees are paid.
d. employees are trained.

2 _______ 10. In order to link pay and performance, high-performance work systems often include some type of
a. glass ceiling.
b. employee incentives.
c. process audit.
d. external fit.

2 _______ 11. By paying employees on the basis of the number of different job skills they have, high-performance work systems may also incorporate
a. piece-rate plans.
b. standard-hour plans.
c. performance evaluation.
d. skill-based pay plans.

2 _______ 12. In addition to linking pay and performance, high-performance work systems are based on the principle of
a. egalitarianism.
b. process auditing.
c. cross-functional training.
d. internal fit.

2 _______ 13. Managers and supervisors in high-performance work systems have the following roles, *except*
a. coaches.
b. facilitators.
c. authoritarian leaders.
d. integrators of team efforts.

2 _______ 14. An addition to the framework of high-performance work systems, vital to business performance is
a. centralized management organizations.
b. rigid organization structures.
c. authoritarian leadership.
d. communication and information technologies.

2

_______ 15. High-performance work systems cannot succeed without accurate and timely information, which includes the following, *except*
a. business plans and goals.
b. deprivation of core competencies.
c. unit and corporate operating results.
d. incipient problems and opportunities.

3

_______ 16. The condition that exists when all internal elements of the work system complement and reinforce each other is
a. job enlargement.
b. external fit.
c. job analysis.
d. internal fit.

3

_______ 17. A strategy that begins with an analysis and discussion of competitive challenges, organizational value, and the concerns of employees and results in a statement of the strategies being pursued by the organization is known as a(n)
a. external fit.
b. process audit.
c. internal fit.
d. job evaluation.

4

_______ 18. A model that helps managers assess the strategic alignment of their work systems is the
a. HR Scorecard.
b. Theory X Model.
c. Theory Y Model.
d. Maslow Model.

4

_______ 19. To get initial commitment to high-performance work systems, managers have to build a case that the changes are needed for the
a. internal fit.
b. external fit.
c. success of the organization.
d. efficiency of the closed system.

4 _______ 20. Autocratic styles of management and confrontational approaches to labor negotiations are being challenged by more enlightened approaches that promote

a. adventurous and technological programs.
b. coercion and communication.
c. cooperation and collaboration.
d. conflict and coordination.

4 _______ 21. In order to establish an alliance, managers and labor representatives should try to create a(n)

a. adversarial system.
b. "win-win" situation.
c. balance-sheet approach.
d. "win-lose" approach.

4 _______ 22. Most labor-management alliances are made legitimate through some tangible symbol of a(n)

a. informal commitment.
b. culture icon.
c. trade agreement.
d. formal commitment.

4 _______ 23. An effective means of ensuring that democracy and fairness prevail, which also keeps the parties focused, is

a. coercion.
b. conflict.
c. command performance.
d. procedure.

4 _______ 24. One of the mistakes that organizations can make in implementing high-performance work systems is

a. effective communication.
b. allocating too few resources to the effort.
c. cooperation and trust.
d. recognition and respect.

4

_______ 25. In which of the following types of firms is building a transition structure least cumbersome?
a. start-up firms
b. growth firms
c. mature firms
d. declining firms

4

_______ 26. The evaluation process that focuses on whether the high-performance work system has been implemented as designed is
a. internal fit.
b. performance appraisal.
c. process audit.
d. external fit.

4

_______ 27. The advantage of high-performance work systems is that they are
a. flexible and adaptable.
b. autocratic and coercive.
c. divisive in conflict.
d. manipulative and confrontational.

5

_______ 28. The following are organizational outcomes that result from using high-performance work systems, *except*
a. lower productivity.
b. lower costs.
c. better responsiveness to customers.
d. higher profitability.

5

_______ 29. High-performance work system outcomes can be categorized in terms of either employee concerns or
a. quality-of-work-life issues
b. job security
c. competitive challenges
d. return on investment

5

_______ 30. Organizations can create a sustainable competitive advantage though people if they focus on four criteria. One of the criteria is
a. difficult to organize
b. cheap
c. easy to find
d. difficult to imitate.

True/False

Identify the following statements as True or False.

1 _______ 1. Without timely and accurate information about the business, employees can do little more than simply carry out orders and perform their roles in a relatively perfunctory way.

1 _______ 2. When employees are given timely information about business performance, plans, and strategies, they are more likely to make good suggestions for improving the business and to cooperate in major organizational changes.

1 _______ 3. Employees in high-performance work systems need to learn in "real time," on the job, using traditional approaches to solve novel problems.

1 _______ 4. A time-tested adage of management is that the interests of employees and organizations naturally diverge.

1 _______ 5. Productivity can improve when introducing egalitarianism by having people who once worked in opposition begin to work together.

2 _______ 6. High-performance work systems combine various work structures, human resources practices, and management processes to maximize employee performance and well-being.

2 _______ 7. Total quality management and reengineering have driven many organizations to redesign their workflow by focusing on the key business processes that drive voluntary layoffs.

2 _______ 8. Work redesign, in and of itself, does not constitute a high-performance work system.

2 _______ 9. Recruitment tends to be both broad and intensive in order to create the best pool of job candidates.

2 _______ 10. Training is focused on ensuring that employees have the skills needed to assume greater responsibility in a high-performance work environment.

2 _______ 11. Because high-performance work systems ask many different things from employees, it is easy to isolate one single compensation approach that works for everyone.

2 _______ 12. The open-pay plan is yet another way to create a more egalitarian environment that discourages employee involvement and commitment.

2 _______ 13. In a growing number of organizations, leadership is shared among team members.

2 _______ 14. The richest form of communication occurs face-to-face between sender and receiver.

2 _______ 15. High-performance work systems can succeed without timely and accurate communications.

3 _______ 16. External fit occurs when all the internal elements of the work system complement and reinforce one another.

3 _______ 17. A situation in which the high-performance work system supports the organization's goals and strategies is known as internal fit.

4 _______ 18. One of the best ways to communicate the business's needs is to show employees the business's current performance and capabilities.

4 _______ 19. Two-way communication can result in better decisions, and it may help to diminish the fears and concerns of employees.

4 _______ 20. Building commitment to high-performance work systems is a one-time activity.

4 _______ 21. The bottom-up approach communicates manager support and clarity, while the top-down approach ensures employee acceptance and commitment.

5 _______ 22. A potential benefit to employees from high-performance work systems is they are likely to be more satisfied and find that their needs for growth are more fully met.

5 _______ 23. Implementing high-performance work systems is an easy task, even though systems are complex, and they require a good deal of close partnering among executives, line managers, HR professionals, union representatives, and employees.

5 _______ 24. Because high-performance work systems are simple to implement, organizations that are successful are simple to copy.

6 _______ 25. The philosophies, principles, and techniques that underlie high-performance work systems are equally appropriate to the management of small and medium-sized organizations.

Matching

Match each term with the proper definition.

Terms

a. external fit
b. high-performance work system (HPWS)
c. internal fit
d. process audit

Definitions

_______ 1. situation in which all the internal elements of the work system complement and reinforce one another

_______ 2. situation in which the work system supports the organization's goals and strategies

_______ 3. specific combination of HR practices, work structures, and processes that maximizes employee knowledge, skill, commitment, and flexibility

_______ 4. determining whether the high-performance work system has been implemented as designed

Internet Exercises

How to manage machine downtime to be more cost effective.
http://www.findarticles.com/p/articles/mi_qa3713/is_200404/ai_n9398989.

What is the result of a high-performance work system in the insurance industry?
http://www.findarticles.com/p/articles/mi_qa3615/is_200504/ai_n13616468.

How to Apply High-Performance Work Systems to Small-, Medium-, and Large-Scale Organizations

High-performance work systems (HPWSs) have become a recent trend for organizations in order to become more efficient and profitable. HPWSs can be defined as a specific combination of human resources practices, work structures, and processes that maximize employee knowledge, skill, commitment, and flexibility. The principles of HPWS apply in small and medium-sized organizational work settings as well as in large organizations. For example, progressive organizations of all sizes have successfully implemented team-based work systems, adopted staffing practices that select high-quality employees, developed training programs that continually update employee skills, and utilized compensation practices that support specific organizational goals. The important element is that these organizations have accomplished these tasks in a coordinated and integrative manner. In smaller organizations, a system approach to organizational design is adopted to combine human resources practices, work structures, and processes that effectively utilize employee competencies. In these small businesses, the human resources function is the responsibility of line management. The line manager must recruit and select among a pool of talent, orient and train these individuals, and assume many of the human resources functions. As the organization grows, the staff function of human resources management becomes a reality for the human resources department that accepts the responsibilities that have been developed in this course.

Regardless of the organization's size, evidence suggests that the use of high-performance work systems has led to increased profitability. Research has shown that human resources practices are aggressive activities that create a stronger competitive advantage relative to other firms. Today, the human resources plan is an integrative approach in developing a holistic system with other departments of small, medium-sized, and large organizations. An objective is to recruit and select the most qualified individuals to perform the necessary tasks to achieve organizational goals.

SOLUTIONS

Multiple Choice:

1. a
2. c
3. c
4. b
5. b
6. d
7. a
8. c
9. a
10. b
11. d
12. a
13. c
14. d
15. b
16. d
17. a
18. a
19. c
20. c
21. b
22. d
23. d
24. b
25. a
26. c
27. a
28. a
29. c
30. d

True/False:

1. True
2. True
3. False
4. True
5. True
6. True
7. False
8. True
9. True
10. True
11. False
12. False
13. True
14. True
15. False
16. False
17. False
18. True
19. True
20. False
21. False
22. True
23. False
24. False
25. True

Matching:

1. c
2. a
3. b
4. d

False Statements Made True

3. Employees in high-performance work systems need to learn in "real time," on the job, using **innovative new** approaches to solve novel problems.
7. Total quality management and reengineering have driven many organizations to redesign their workflow by focusing on the key business processes that drive **customer value**.

11. Because high-performance work systems ask many different things from employees, it is **difficult** to isolate one single compensation approach that works for everyone.
12. The open-pay plan is yet another way to create a more egalitarian environment that **encourages** employee involvement and commitment.
15. High-performance work systems **cannot** succeed without timely and accurate communications.
16. **Internal** fit occurs when all the internal elements of the work system complement and reinforce one another.
17. A situation in which the high-performance work system supports the organization's goals and strategies is known as **external** fit.
20. Building commitment to high-performance work systems is **an ongoing** activity.
21. The **top-down** approach communicates manager support and clarity, while the **bottom-up** approach ensures employee acceptance and commitment.
23. Implementing high-performance work systems is **a difficult** task **because** systems are complex, and they require a good deal of close partnering among executives, line managers, HR professionals, union representatives, and employees.
24. Because high-performance work systems are **difficult** to implement, organizations that are successful are **difficult** to copy.